TIPS AND OTHER BRIGHT IDEAS

for Secondary School Libraries

Volume Three
Sherry York, Editor

Linworth Books

Professional Development Resources for
K-12 Library Media and Technology Specialists

Library of Congress Cataloging-in-Publication Data

Tips and other bright ideas for secondary school librarians. Volume 3/Sherry York, editor.
    p. cm.
Continues: Tips, ideas for secondary school librarians & technology specialists. 2nd ed.
c2000.
Includes bibliographical references and index.
    ISBN 1-58683-210-7 (alk. paper)
1. High school libraries--United States--Administration.   I. York,
    Sherry, 1947- . II. Tips, ideas for secondary school librarians & technology specialists.

Z675.S3T4945 2005
025.1'978--dc22

                              2005029594

Published by Linworth Publishing, Inc.
480 East Wilson Bridge road, Suite L
Worthington, Ohio 43085

Copyright ©2006 by Linworth Publishing, Inc.

ISBN 1-58683-210-7

TABLE
OF CONTENTS

INTRODUCTION

Much has happened since the earlier editions of *Tips*. The first volume was published in 1991 as *Tips and Other Bright Ideas for School Librarians*. The second volume in 2000 was *Tips: Ideas for Secondary School Librarians & Technology Specialists*. These past fifteen years have seen many changes in the world of school libraries.

In 1991 there was *The Book Report*. In 2000, you were sending tips to *The Book Report*, but in January 2003, *The Book Report* and *Library Talk* became *Library Media Connection*. August 2006 will see the start of volume 25 of *Library Media Connection*—twenty-five years of librarians learning from each other and sharing the wealth of information. During those years we have seen personal computers become commonplace. Enormous changes have occurred in technology and in school libraries.

Paradoxically, much has not changed since 1991 and 2000. Librarians in 2006 manage their libraries and consider furniture, arrangement, signage, and overall appearance of the facility. We try to keep things in order and provide supplies and equipment to meet the needs of students and teachers. Books and materials must still be processed. Budgets are seldom generous enough for us to acquire all the things we want to provide. We are continually planning for, putting up, and replacing displays and bulletin boards to advertise our wares.

Twenty-first-century school librarians work with students, teachers, and staff always promoting reading, teaching research skills, and building positive public relations. We still check materials and equipment in and out and work to keep the library media center interesting and attractive. We use technology to do all these things and more on a daily basis. We train student helpers, work with volunteers, attend conferences and workshops, connect with parents and the public, and in a multitude of ways make valuable contributions to the education of our youth.

With the advent of No Child Left Behind and tightened accountability, school librarians are, more than ever, aware of the need for integrating curriculum and establishing collaborative relationships with teachers. We have embraced technology and used technology to make our work more efficient, to teach students and teachers, to promote reading, and to build positive public relations.

Dire predictions of the demise of libraries and prognostications of a paperless society have not materialized. Better quality, more relevant books are being published, more children are being educated, and school librarians are eternally working to bring books and students together so that the power of learning and literature will continue.

Secondary school librarians and technology specialists are usually on the lookout for ways to do more and to do their multifaceted jobs more efficiently. The tips on the following pages should help!

Tips in this book are categorized into nine sections:

- Managing the Library
- Working with Students in the Library
- Teaching Research Skills
- Collaborating with Teachers
- Using Technology in the Library
- Promoting Reading
- Building Positive Public Relations
- Working with Helpers
- Managing Tips for the Librarian

We at Linworth are grateful for your loyal readership for these twenty plus years and for the generosity of secondary school librarians who are always willing to share. As you read these tips, you may say to yourself, "I do that too" or "I've always done that." Perhaps you will also think, "Wow! That gives me an idea." When you have those wow moments, take a few minutes to write up a tip or two and send them to *Library Media Connection*. It pays—a little cash and a great feeling of having contributed to the betterment of our profession!

MANAGING
THE
LIBRARY

School libraries are multi-use places. The capable school librarian is responsible for overseeing all physical aspects of the library media center. Decisions about arrangement of the library, furniture, and signage should contribute toward making it a functional, accessible, attractive, and comfortable space.

Managing the library involves keeping the area clean and uncluttered and maintaining order among library materials. Some thoughtful librarians provide supplies for students to use in and out of the library. Many are responsible for checking audio-visual equipment to teachers. The librarian processes new books and materials and often finds ingenious ways to acquire more materials for the collection. Last, but not least, the library media specialist provides interesting, intriguing displays and bulletin boards.

This section of tips includes the following topics:

- Arrangement
- Furniture
- Signage
- Appearance
- Maintaining Order
- Supplies
- Equipment
- Processing Books and Materials
- Acquisitions
- Displays
- Bulletin Boards

ARRANGEMENT

Assistive Student

To build up one of our students with cerebral palsy and to save myself time, I asked a student to borrow a wheel chair as part of his grade level project. He then tried to navigate our library and noted on a map areas that were difficult or impossible for him to negotiate. He tried out our tables, desks, counters, and the length of cord on our keyboards. Another student has been asked to label things in Braille. Encouraging students to be analytical and compassionate about assistive devices and accessibility issues has had great dividends for them and for the library. Plus we are now more prepared to be hospitable (and legal).

Sheryl Kindle Fullner, Nooksack Valley Middle School, Everson, Washington
Library Media Connection • March 2004 (Volume 22, Issue 6)

Poetry Corner

To celebrate Poetry Month in April, try emptying your magazine display stand, then moving it and your leisure furniture to a remote corner of the library media center. Fill the display with poetry books, local poetry contest fliers, and student-authored haiku poetry bookmarks. Get science or social studies teachers involved by having their students write a haiku on something they have studied this year. Students can come to this Poetry Corner during lunch or common time to read their original poetry and listen to other's poetry. Then, when May arrives, transform this corner into the Battle of the Books meeting area. Place all the new Battle of the Books titles in the magazine rack to promote a summer reading program. It becomes a place where students can read the covers, meet the present Battle of the Books team members to discuss the new titles for the coming year, and ask each other questions.

Gay Ann Loesch, Sun Valley Middle, Indian Trail, North Carolina
Library Media Connection • March 2005 (Volume 23, Issue 6)

I Can See Clearly, Now

When redesigning a library, be sure to angle all shelving so that you can see between the rows from the charge desk.

Ann Patterson, Lindsay Middle School, Hampton, Virginia
The Book Report • March/April 2002 (Volume 20, Issue 5)

No Peeking!

To create cozy reading areas within the larger space of the library media center, hang a juvenile shower curtain using clear monofilament line from the ceiling until the bottom of the curtain is near floor level. Put out a selection of books and other media that tie in with the subject. The curtains are often available at discount stores for under $5 and provide lots of vivid color with no effort. So far we have used a saltwater aquarium scene, frolicking unicorns, and racecars.

Sheryl Fullner, Nooksack Valley Middle School, Everson, Washington
Library Media Connection • October 2005 (Volume 24, Issue 2)

Cappuccino to Go

Are you thinking of adding a cappuccino bar to your library, but not sure that it will work for you? Why not try negotiating with a local convenience store to borrow one for a few days? The slowest time for many businesses is during school hours, so finding a business that is willing to work with you may be easier than you think. Offer to move the machine, pay for the product, and split the profits. Or approach the project as a fundraiser for your library and ask them to donate the product. Either way, you will be able to determine whether or not a cappuccino bar is the right addition for your library.

Brook Berg, Detroit Lakes (Minnesota) Middle School
Library Media Connection • March 2006 (Volume 24, Issue 6)

Moving a Library

If you have to move a library for new carpet and painting, before you pack the first book, label the shelf by writing on a sheet of paper in large letters the call numbers of the books on that shelf, from beginning to the end of the shelf. Make two labels, one at the beginning of the shelf and one at the end of the shelf. Be sure to tape down the labels securely. If shelves have to be removed from your stacks, place a small piece of masking tape under the shelf before you remove the shelf. This will let you know where to place the shelf when you move back into the library. Label each box of books to match the labels on the shelf. By doing this, books can be placed on the shelves as one comes to the box. Boxes do not have to be in Dewey order. These hints will save time moving back into the library.

Nancy Keenan, Glenvar High School, Roanoke (Virginia) County School
Library Media Connection • August/September 2004 (Volume 23, Issue 1)

FURNITURE

Comfortable Library Seating

To make the library more accessible and comfortable to teenagers, I looked to local bookstores for decorating ideas. I bought some secondhand easy chairs, each under $30, from Goodwill and antique malls. Getting into the spirit of it, our principal made an announcement that teachers and parents who were redecorating could donate their old furniture to the library. That gained us four more wingback chairs. Students and teachers love the comfortable seating, and we've reached students who never before hung out in the library.

Laura Younkin, Ballard High School, Louisville, Kentucky
The Book Report • January/February 2001 (Volume 19, Issue 4)

Glider Rockers

To promote leisure reading and better access to our fiction collection, we purchased three glider rockers. These rockers, coupled with a side table and a lamp, make our reading area quite popular with our students and teachers. Before and after school and at lunch, patrons rock away, enjoying our newspapers, magazines, and fiction books. Additionally, many of our teachers are displaced from their classrooms during their planning periods, so they relax in the rockers while they grade papers and prepare lessons. An added benefit is providing us additional opportunities to collaborate with these teachers. Also, the rockers are the most popular seats in the house during faculty meetings!

Ann Bryant and Libby Bagby, North Surry High School, Mt. Airy, North Carolina
Library Media Connection • February 2004 (Volume 22, Issue 5)

Window Seating

To bring seating up to required levels without taking up floor space or purchasing expensive tables, we put an 18-inch wide, laminate-covered plywood counter under our windows. It is supported with simple knee braces of two by four lumber. Twelve high stools attract students as does the sunlight in winter. The counters also face our bird feeding areas and feature used binoculars and birding books.

 Sheryl Kindle Fullner, Nooksack Valley Middle School, Everson, Washington
Library Media Connection • August/September 2004 (Volume 23, Issue 1)

"New" Furniture

The modern industrial or loft look of stainless steel is very appealing but out of our budget range. Our school had several old steel desks with pink or pale green drawers. Stripping furniture obviously is not in our job description, but stripping flat-front metal furniture is a cinch with industrial-strength stripper. My desk drawers took less than an hour. Now with a bit of beeswax, the whole desk looks upscale!

 Sheryl Kindle Fullner, Nooksack Valley Middle School, Everson, Washington
Library Media Connection • February 2006 (Volume 24, Issue 5)

SIGNAGE

High Visibility Signage

To create high visibility signage that blends in with library furnishings, type the sign in a large, clear font and then copy it onto a transparency. Signs should measure smaller than 3 inches high. Use four-inch clear library tape to attach the trimmed sign wherever it is needed. Use this method to indicate Dewey ranges on the ends of shelves and the contents of cabinets. Every year or so when the numbers may change, the signs easily peel off, and any excess gumminess can be quickly removed with rubber cement thinner. This method allows the color of the furniture to show through and is far quicker, with more options, than a label maker.

Sheryl Fullner, Nooksack Valley Middle School, Everson, Washington
Library Media Connection • November/December 2005 (Volume 24, Issue 3)

MS Word Label Making

We have several special collections in our media center. To designate which books belong in those collections, we have designed collection labels using Microsoft Word's label-making capability. We select a graphic and replicate it three times on a standard address label. Underneath each of the graphics, we place codes, such as CAREER, ATLAS, DICTIONARY, etc. We copy the single label to fill the entire sheet and print it on a color printer. The paper cutter makes nice, clean cuts between the designs on the label. We now have far fewer items shelved in the wrong collection.

Linda Kelso Hicks, Portage (Indiana) High School-East
The Book Report • January/February 2000 (Volume 18, Issue 4)

Hold Your Place

If you have no room to display signs showing the location of books, create inexpensive markers that fit within the shelves. Use the flyer option in Publisher® to create signs designating the Dewey divisions. Laminate the signs and glue them to plastic magazine holders. Students will be able to see the general book locations from across the library media center.

Shelly Burnside, Brownstown (Indiana) Central High School
Library Media Connection • February 2006 (Volume 24, Issue 5)

Student-Created Dewey Posters

At the beginning of the school year, I hand out to groups of students sheets of poster board cut in half vertically. They are assigned a range of Dewey numbers such as 500-550 and given a glue stick along with a pile of old magazines. They go to an Internet site that describes Dewey numbers and then look for items to clip out to illustrate their numbers. Cooperative social and leadership skills come into play as they divide up the work. They print out large fancy numbers on the word processor and glue them near the pictures with the lowest number at the top as they work their way down the board. This project is more fun and cheaper than ordering Dewey posters for mounting on shelving endcaps or suspending from our ceiling on monofilament line.

Sheryl Kindle Fullner, Nooksack Valley Middle School, Everson, Washington
The Book Report • September/October 2001 (Volume 20, Issue 2)

APPEARANCE

Right Tool for the Right Job

Purchase handheld appliances at garage sales and keep them in the back room of the LMC.

A curling iron can be used for smoothing and refreshing all kinds of bows, ribbons, streamers, and flags. Purchase a travel iron for pressing creases out of banners and paper posters. A hair dryer is useful for speeding up the drying of paint on LMC projects and for drying cloth after a spill is cleaned up. And an electric drill is great for stirring paint. Having the right tool at hand for the job makes it easy to delegate that job. (And of course, with the exception of the drill, they can always be used for gussying up the Librarian, male or female.)

 Sheryl Kindle Fullner, Nooksack Valley Middle School, Everson, Washington
Library Media Connection • November/December 2004 (Volume 23, Issue 3)

Art in the Library

Our library has ceiling tiles that aren't particularly pleasant to look at. By cooperating with our art teachers, we allowed senior art students to borrow a ceiling tile and decorate it. When they are done we place the tiles back into the ceiling. This way, our library slowly gets an artistic make-over, and senior art students leave behind a lasting legacy. Almost everyone who enters the library enjoys this unusual art form. Students return every year to see their works of art! *Editor's note:* be sure to get permission from the student to eventually destroy the art when the tile gets stained or worn.

 Steven Reed, Wilmington (Ohio) High School
Library Media Connection • March 2006 (Volume 24, Issue 6)

"Designer" Magazine Files

Since the magazine files may be visible to everyone, aesthetics really do matter. To solve the problem of ugly files, purchase pretty self-stick wallpaper border in a width that covers the narrow, shorter front of the file box. After washing the dust off the old boxes, apply the border to the fronts of the boxes. You may wish to decorate not only the boxes but also the fronts of old file cabinets, and the top fronts of bookcases that hold the file boxes. The patterned border can tie old, disparately colored furnishings together for a lovely custom look.

Jane Thompson, Ludlow (Massachusetts) High School
The Book Report • May/June 2001 (Volume 20, Issue 1)

Removing Permanent Marker

If students get permanent marker on the tables or someone accidentally uses a permanent marker on a dry erase board, you can remove it by taking a dry erase marker and running it over the permanent marks. Finish with a damp wet cloth. Works every time.

Joe Holmes, Weston, Florida
Library Media Connection • April/May 2006 (Volume 24, Issue 7)

Coffee Filters

Simple white coffee filters are versatile and handy in the library. Dampen one slightly with glass cleaner and use it to clean computer monitors. Dampen slightly with water and use to clean laser printers. Remove the toner cartridge and carefully wipe off any rollers inside the printer that may accumulate lint and dust. Use dry filters to clean microscope and digital camera lenses and viewfinders. The coffee filters are so effective because they are lint-free.

Janice Gumerman, Bingham 7th Grade Center, Independence, Missouri
Library Media Connection • February 2005 (Volume 23, Issue 5)

Stain Remover

Remove permanent marker from whiteboards using rubbing alcohol. It works because the ink is alcohol-based, and it will not ruin the finish on the whiteboard.

Some cheaper hairsprays with high alcohol content may also work, but may also leave a sticky residue. Rubbing alcohol can also be used to remove ballpoint ink from tables, computer keyboards and monitors, and some fabrics.

Amy Johnston, Swift Current Comprehensive High School,
  Swift Current, SK, Canada
Library Media Connection • March 2004 (Volume 22, Issue 6)

Festive Paper and Pencil Holders

Each season or holiday, decorate the library with appropriate items to create a festive atmosphere. Part of the decorations can include small, sturdy plastic cups with holiday imprints. These are purchased very inexpensively, no more than $1.00 for four. Placed by each computer workstation, they are very effective and decorative paper and pencil holders that add nicely to the seasonal themes. They are easy to store and to replace if necessary.

Janice Gumerman, Bingham 7th Grade Center, Independence, Missouri
Library Media Connection • November/December 2005 (Volume 24, Issue 3)

"Posting" Information about Your Book Fair

The posters that sell as part of the Book Fair are hot items. Many library media specialists display them inside the library media center; another idea is to tape them to the library media center windows facing out, so that kids see them as they walk around the building. This is an extra way to tantalize students to come into the library media center! I also use the posters as prizes throughout the year.

Laura Stiles, Cedar Valley Middle School, Austin, Texas
Library Media Connection • October 2005 (Volume 24, Issue 2)

Uses for Old CDs

Catch students' eyes and attention by using old CDs for library media center decorations. Collect and save advertising and out-of-date CDs. Use sticky tape to stick CDs directly on media center walls. Be sure to mount them with the shiny sides facing out. Or, you can use rubber cement to make CDs part of a bulletin board display. Use string to suspend CDs (back-to-back) from the library media center ceiling. Not only do the CD displays get students' attention, they are also quick and easy to create.

Deb Logan, Taft Middle School, Marion, Ohio
The Book Report • November/December 2000 (Volume 19, Issue 3)

Table Doily

If your LMC is the location for your school's hospitality (luncheons, teas, meetings, etc.), you can dress it up quickly for some of the more special occasions. Fold a yard and a half of colored butcher paper in quarters. Three quick wiggly scissor cuts (one to take out the center, one midway, and one around the outside edge) turn the paper into a giant doily for your tables. One centers each large double table. Visitors will comment on how festive it looks, and the cost in time and materials is negligible.

Sheryl Kindle Fullner, Nooksack Valley Middle School, Everson, Washington
Library Media Connection • November/December 2003 (Volume 22, Issue 3)

MAINTAINING
ORDER

Keeping Paperbacks in Place

To keep paperback books forward on the shelf, I buy the plastic corner strips that you can purchase at discount and hardware stores to keep wallpaper safe and secure on corners. I cut them to fit the shelves and use double stick tape to keep them in place.

Lynette Mitchell, Withlacoochee Technical Institute, Inverness, Florida
The Book Report • September/October 2001 (Volume 20, Issue 2)

Organizing Company Catalogs

To organize vendor catalogs, use a permanent Sharpie® pen (this writes on all types of covers) to label the catalog. On the top left of the front cover, I write the name of the company. On the top middle, I write the type of catalog. On the top right, I put the date the catalog was received. File these in Princeton magazine files labeled with the following categories: A-V Equipment, Book Sale, Foreign Language, Computer, Library Publisher, Library Supplies, Multimedia (all types of formats), Prebound and Paperback, School Supplies, Textbook and Instructional, Vertical File, and Video or DVD. Within each file, arrange the catalogs in alphabetical order by company name. When a new catalog is received, throw away the old one and replace it with the new one. Writing the date received shows you if the catalog is current and helps when weeding the out-of-date ones.

Dorothy Pope, Lawrence County High School, Lawrenceburg, Tennessee
Library Media Connection • January 2006 (Volume 24, Issue 4)

Newspapers in Order

Our newspapers are always cumbersome, messy piles in our storeroom. We purchase masonite boards, cut them for dividers and label them for the month and a couple of sets of days on two sides. The newspapers are filed now with the correct months and the latest two with the dates. Students going "digging" for articles specific to dates have left us with neat piles ready for the next researchers. The huge dividers really work.

Jane Cabaya, Century High School, Rochester, Minnesota
Library Media Connection • January 2003 (Volume 21, Issue 4)

Catalog Control

Set up a small table as a catalog order desk with plastic Princeton files lined up and labeled with the alphabet. As each catalog arrives it only takes a moment to compare it with its mates in the file and discard either a duplicate or the superseded issue. You do not need to keep the individual catalogs in exact order within the files because it is easy to spot sister catalogs by their spines.

Sheryl Kindle Fullner, Nooksack Valley Middle School, Everson, Washington
Library Media Connection • October 2004 (Volume 23, Issue 2)

Magazine Theft

I had a problem with students walking out with certain magazines so I put barcode labels on file folders and keep them in a file cabinet at the desk. Students pick out the magazine they want, I check the folder out and keep it at the desk, then check it back in when the magazine is returned. This has cut down on the thefts 100 percent.

Harolyn Legg, Liberty-Benton High School, Findlay, Ohio
The Book Report • September/October 2000 (Volume 19, Issue 2)

SUPPLIES

Supplies on the Spot

I purchased a small plastic multi-drawer organizer that I place on top of my desk. Students are free to borrow anything in any of the drawers. I have a drawer with pencils, another with highlighters, and one with glue sticks, scissors, rubber bands, and correction fluid. On top of my counter, I keep a three-hole punch and a stapler handy as well. A bucket of crayons and a box of markers and colored pencils are also within easy reach. Rulers, which double as space savers for the younger set, are in a box nearby. Now I don't have to continuously jump up from what I am doing to go and get materials that students need to complete their projects.

 Ann M. G. Gray, Pittsburg (New Hampshire) School Media Center
Library Media Connection • April/May 2005 (Volume 23, Issue 7)

The Shoe Bank

Students often ask to borrow non-media items from the library: a yardstick, scissors, a stapler, etc. Because I don't know each of our hundreds of students by name, I have them leave one shoe near my desk. When the items are returned, the students take back their shoe. Even the most forgetful student doesn't get on the bus with one shoe.

 Sheryl Kindle Fullner, Nooksack Valley Middle School, Everson, Washington
Library Media Connection • April/May 2003 (Volume 21, Issue 7)

Everything's Coming Up Pencils

Do the pens and pencils you loan to students never return? Here's a simple solution. You will need a cheap plastic vase, a few fake flowers, and a roll of green tape. Cut the blooms off at the stems, and tape them to the tops of your pens and pencils. Arrange them in the vase, and place it on your library circulation counter. When students ask to borrow a pen or pencil, tell them they are welcome to use any of the flower pens or pencils. You will find that pens and pencils are returned every time! An added advantage is that it will brighten up your desk. Tip: Use smaller (lighter weight) flowers to make writing easier.

Amy Johnston, Swift Current Comprehensive High School,
    Saskatchewan, Canada
Library Media Connection • February 2004 (Volume 22, Issue 5)

Ordering Supplies

Our district orders most supplies from a large consortium. Instead of limiting myself to the library/stationery sections of the catalog, I use the whole book to order items such as eight-inch forceps (tweezers), individual alcohol towelettes, and a box of latex examination gloves. The tweezers are excellent for printer paper jams. The towelettes are great for sticky keyboards. The gloves will last through several years of student painting/decorating projects in the library. Small convenience items such as these, which might not get budget approval on an individual purchase order, are readily approved in this mass order.

Sheryl Kindle Fullner, Nooksack Valley Middle School, Everson, Washington
Library Media Connection • April/May 2004 (Volume 22, Issue 7)

Check It Out!

Have problems keeping track of miscellaneous items such as the bathroom pass or markers and pencils? We did—until we slapped a barcode on such items and checked them out to students! Supplies must be used in the library, but students are held accountable for their return. It also helps keep track of how long students are out on bathroom passes.

Liz Sargent, Palatine (Illinois) High School
Library Media Connection • January 2005 (Volume 23, Issue 4)

Emergency Batteries

Keep some small (AA) batteries on hand for teacher emergencies. These are the size that fit small flashlights and some classroom games as well as various school cameras. Most disposable cameras come with a battery inside. We stop by our local film processors and ask for a bag of these used batteries for our library. There is usually lots of life left in them and they are free.

Sheryl Kindle Fullner, Nooksack Valley Middle School, Everson, Washington
Library Media Connection • January 2004 (Volume 22, Issue 4)

EQUIPMENT

Scheduling TV/VCR/DVD Units

Scheduling TV/VCR/DVD units can be a nightmare for librarians. In order to eliminate confusion and simplify the process, create a signup slip that teachers fill out with their requests. Include a spot for the teacher's name, the dates, and class periods the unit is needed, and if there is any special request, i.e., they must have a DVD unit for their presentation. From this sign-up slip, prepare the schedule. This slip will also serve as a way of double checking the schedule. Be sure to include a statement on the slips that says, "The player is being used for curricular purposes" in order to cover copyright issues.

Ruth Riley, Poland (Ohio) Seminary High School
Library Media Connection • April/May 2005 (Volume 23, Issue 7)

Barcoding Library Equipment

I barcoded all our library's TVs, VCRs, and their respective remotes. Our barcode labels came with a smaller sticker with the same number. I put the small sticker on the remote and the barcode label on the VCR or TV. The TV and cart also each have their own barcode. When a teacher checks out a cart, TV, and VCR, I need to check out three items.

David Lininger, Hickory County R-1 Schools, Urbana, Missouri
The Book Report • September/October 2001 (Volume 20, Issue 2)

Barcode Equipment Too

Track audiovisual equipment through the automated circulation system. Barcode and catalog all equipment and check it out using your system. If a piece of equipment is missing you can easily see who last checked it out. Use the automation software's report feature to run monthly statistics and see which items have been heavily used.

 Jenni Seibel, DC Everest Middle School, Weston, Wisconsin
Library Media Connection • August/September 2004 (Volume 23, Issue 1)

AV Cookbook

Teachers and staff sometimes have a hard time running audiovisual equipment that they do not use often. To solve this problem, create an Audiovisual Electronic Cookbook for your school. Use a digital camera to take pictures of all the steps of how to use equipment, insert them into a PowerPoint slide show, and add the text. Once the slide show is completed, link it to your school's Web site or your library media center page so teachers and staff always have access to it.

 Laura Jeanette Brown, Paint Branch High School, Burtonsville, Maryland
Library Media Connection • October 2005 (Volume 24, Issue 2)

Smile!

For equipment with multiple pieces, take a digital photo of the item and all of the accessories that go with it. Using word processing software, import the photo and label all of the pieces. Include this guide in the bag or case with the equipment. Teachers can see what needs to be returned and check to make sure it is included. It helps the library staff also!

 Jenni Seibel, D.C. Everest Middle School, Weston, Wisconsin
Library Media Connection • October 2004 (Volume 23, Issue 2)

"Time" to Remember

Ever had a teacher stop you in the hall, the office, or during lunch and ask you to do this or that? Maybe they tell you they need a video or a bulb. You hear yourself say, "Sure," as you smile and wonder, "How will I remember that?" If you wear a watch, move it from one wrist to the other. Think about what you need to remember while moving the watch. Do not let yourself move the watch back to its normal and more comfortable spot until you have handled the request.

Debra Kay Logan, Taft Middle School, Marion, Ohio
The Book Report • January/February 2001 (Volume 19, Issue 4)

Use for Old Equipment

After I automated my circulation several years ago, I was left with a Gaylord Model C Book Charger. Rather than retire the machine, I use it to stamp book marks, then use the marks as date dues on special occasions.

Joy Harrison, Buffalo (Missouri) High School
The Book Report • May/June 2000 (Volume 19, Issue 1)

Control the Remotes

I put half of a Velcro strip on the bottom of our television remote controls and the other half on the bottom of the shelf holding the TV so that it's hardly visible when attached. This system really helps keep the remotes from "walking away."

Dawne Wheeler Reed, Hohokam Middle School, Tucson, Arizona
The Book Report • January/February 2002 (Volume 20, Issue 4)

A Gaggle of Remotes

To store remote controls when not in use, buy a hanging plastic shoe rack and label each pocket for the appropriate VCR/TV. Pop the remotes in their pockets and you will always know where they are.

Deb Mabbott, Centralia (Washington) High School
Library Media Connection • October 2003 (Volume 22, Issue 2)

VCR Troubleshooting Guide

If you are frequently called into the classroom to troubleshoot TV/VCR problems, try posting a troubleshooting guide on the VCR. We list the basics, such as "Check to make sure channel is set to 3," and "Check to make sure that the back of the VCR cable is connected to 'video out' on the VCR and to 'video in' on the back of the TV." The guide is laminated and then taped to the top of the VCR, where it is readily visible.

Jane Perry, Winslow Jr. High Library, St. Winslow, Maine
The Book Report • September/October 2001 (Volume 20, Issue 2)

Hair Ties

To keep all the assorted equipment cords neat and tidy, pull them together with hair ties. If you used rubber bands or twisties, the hair ties are easy to spot, don't break, and are stronger.

Barbara Schiefler, Alvarado Middle School Media Center, Union City, California
Library Media Connection • October 2003 (Volume 22, Issue 2)

Color-coded Cables

If you often check multiple pieces of AV or computer equipment out to the same teacher, to get the correct cords and cables with each piece of equipment, use colored electrical tape to mark all of the cords and cables that belong with one piece of equipment. For example: red for the VCRs, blue for the projectors, and so on. Then you can get the equipment returned with the correct cables and cords!

Jenni Seibel, DC Everest Middle School, Weston, Wisconsin
Library Media Connection • August/September 2004 (Volume 23, Issue 1)

Clip and Roll

The roll laminator you may have in the teachers' workroom tends to curl back on the rollers if one does not watch the document coming out. To alleviate this, attach spring clothespins to the two outer corners of the leading edge. The clothespins weigh down the plastic film just enough so that it does not curl.

Janice Gumerman, Bingham 7th Grade Center, Independence, Missouri
Library Media Connection • October 2003 (Volume 22, Issue 2)

PROCESSING
BOOKS AND MATERIALS

Stamping Your Books

So you won't lose library materials that are returned to the public library and other district schools, invest in a stamp that includes all contact information for your library: name, address, and phone number. At least if a book is misplaced, the finder can contact you, and you have a better chance of retrieving it.

Janice Gumerman, Bingham Middle School, Independence, Missouri
Library Media Connection • April/May 2006 (Volume 24, Issue 7)

Sticky Residue

To remove the adhesive residue left by stickers on book jackets, spray a little Citrus Magic, or other popular citrus-oil product, on the sticky spot and wipe. This not only cleans the area but also makes it smell fresh. Use Spray and Wash to combat the sticky places on desks or wooden closet doors where posters were hung with masking tape.

Sue Popejoy, M. T. Reilly Elementary School, Dallas, Texas
The Book Report • November/December 2002 (Volume 21, Issue 3)

Sticky Situation

Use a drop of lighter fluid (usually used to refill cigarette lighters) to remove the sticky residue often left on books after removing price tags and other stickers.

Amy Johnston, Swift Current Comprehensive High School,
    Swift Current, SK, Canada
Library Media Connection • March 2004 (Volume 22, Issue 6)

Processing Books

If you have a cart or a counter of books being processed, give each book a routing slip to keep track of what has been done and what needs to be done before it can be shelved. This allows any volunteer or student aide to keep busy. This is a sample of our slip which is printed on bright paper.

DO DONE

❏ ❏ property stamp or label
❏ ❏ barcode attach
❏ ❏ mylar cover for jacket
❏ ❏ vinyl for paperback
❏ ❏ find in OPAC, add copy

Call # _____

Sheryl Kindle Fullner, Nooksack Valley Middle School, Everson, Washington
Library Media Connection • March 2004 (Volume 22, Issue 6)

Catalog Clips

When I do original cataloging, it is sometimes difficult to hold a book open to locate the pertinent information for the catalog record. To solve this problem, I use a large "chip clip" that easily clamps down the cover and first few pages to get to the information that I need. A large alligator clip would also work.

Janice Gumerman, Bingham 7th Grade Center, Independence, Missouri
Library Media Connection • August/September 2005 (Volume 24, Issue 1)

Secondary Book Jackets

When book jackets are seriously worn, but the books are still intact, create a new jacket. Photocopy a 11 x 17-inch piece of black and white checked contact paper or a sheet of wrapping paper (so it can be used over and over). Large pieces of brightly colored paper can also be used for the base instead of the checkered copy. If any element of the old jacket is still in good condition, trim it to a rectangle and glue it on the checkered photocopy. Otherwise download the cover from an internet bookstore, print, and glue. Print the title for the spine. Encase all these layers in a mylar jacket along with the barcode and spine label. The freshened books will circulate far more often. If students are handling this project, they may glue on their own review of the book as well. This technique is far more fun than a standard book report.

Sheryl Kindle Fullner, Nooksack Valley Middle School, Everson, Washington
Library Media Connection • January 2004 (Volume 22, Issue 4)

Hot Laminating

Try hot laminating book jackets. Old books that are given new life are far more appealing to prospective readers. Laminated covers protect new books better than regular book jacket covers. Use a hot lamination process, and cut the laminate about two inches beyond the book cover at the top and bottom. Fold this extra laminate to the inside, and tape it in place. Attach to the book by strapping tape.

Ladonna Micko, Mickelson Middle School, Brookings, South Dakota
Library Media Connection • February 2004 (Volume 22, Issue 5)

Book Jacket Uses

Save book jackets from laminated books to display as new books or for an author of the month (if the author or artist visits, ask them to autograph the cover), or for library lessons on authors and titles. You can also turn laminated book jackets into puzzles or bookmarks. Let students decorate lockers and cover textbooks with excess jackets. You could even create borders and columns on the library walls.

Carol Kotsch, St. Elizabeth Ann Seton, Wichita, Kansas
The Book Report • November/December 2002 (Volume 21, Issue 3)

Beware of Book Jacket Hijackers!

Book jackets equal big money in the secondary market, so stealing them can be lucrative. Color photocopy rare jackets (usually for early novels by popular authors) and put these copies on your books. Store the original for safekeeping or sell it on the Internet to collectors to raise money for your library. You can even sell photocopies of rare jackets. Copies offered for sale should be in public domain (published before 1923 or with a lapsed copyright), and it's wise to unobtrusively mark each one as a copy on the unseen back of the jacket.

Sheryl Kindle Fullner, Nooksack Valley Middle School, Everson, Washington
The Book Report • November/December 2001 (Volume 20, Issue 3)

Barcoding Videotapes

When processing videotapes, CDs, and DVDs, write the barcode on the item itself, not just on the case in which it comes. This way, if a borrower loses the box, you can quickly determine the necessary information. You can check in the item and, if necessary, put it in a new box to circulate again.

Katie Sessler, Jackson Middle School Library, Grand Prairie, Texas
Library Media Connection • October 2003 (Volume 22, Issue 2)

ACQUISITIONS

Recruiting New Materials

Many Hi-Lo books are related to the armed forces. Books abound about Marines, Navy Seals, Army Night Commandos, Air Force adventures, and Coast Guard exploits. While these titles were much in demand by my students, I wasn't eager to spend library funds on books that are basically recruitment tools. So, I visited each of our local armed services recruiters in person, armed with a highlighted printout of several books related to their branch of the armed forces, the 800 number for the publisher of same, and our school library address. I asked them if they would donate the selected books to our library. Not only was my request graciously received, but I also returned to school loaded down with mugs, CD cases, lanyards, water bottles, posters, and pens, which were given to students to generate more used book donations. (I did show each recruiter what the previous one had given me to appeal to their competitive spirits.)

Sheryl Kindle Fullner, Nooksack Valley Middle School, Everson, Washington
Library Media Connection • April/May 2003 (Volume 21, Issue 7)

Free Books

Your public library or AAUW (American Association of University Women) or other groups having book sales may allow you to pick up some of the books that are left after their regular book sales. Usually the groups just have to discard the books or bring them to the recycling center. Most of the books are too worn to put in the library, but you can put them on tables in front of the library, and students and staff can help themselves. I save some to put out when we have Parents' Night.

Anitra Gordon, Lincoln High School Library, Ypsilanti, Michigan
Library Media Connection • October 2003 (Volume 22, Issue 2)

Pam File

When filling out postcards or writing letters or e-mail to request information, flyers, pamphlets, posters, or other materials, I always list my name as "Pam File." When the materials come in, I know immediately that the item was requested specifically for my vertical or pamphlet file. It saves time; I can put those items in a pile to process all together at a later time.

Anna Hartle, Cincinnati Country Day School, Cincinnati, Ohio
The Book Report • November/December 2000 (Volume 19, Issue 3)

International News

Although our library is in a rural area, ethnic restaurants abound nearby. We encourage teachers to keep an eye out for any free foreign language newspapers displayed at restaurants. Depending on the cuisine, we have Spanish, Punjabi, and occasionally Japanese periodicals. We use these newspapers to give a world flavor to our magazine area without spending money. Plus they are a nice tool for making our immigrant students feel welcome and included.

Sheryl Kindle Fullner, Nooksack Valley Middle School, Everson, Washington
Library Media Connection • August/September 2004 (Volume 23, Issue 1)

Classroom or Media Center Scrapbook

Invite students to contribute artwork, book reviews, news reports, and other items of interest to a scrapbook. A regular scrapbook or something like a wallpaper sample book can be used to organize the contributions. Be sure each item is dated and contains the contributor's name.

Claudette Hegel, Bloomington, Minnesota
Library Media Connection • January 2003 (Volume 21, Issue 4)

Encyclopedia Yearbooks

The encyclopedia yearbooks are very helpful when students have to do reports on the events of a specific year. I've never purchased them, but some have been donated over the years. Telling staff and students how useful they could be generated additional donations, and I picked up several others at the recycle center. Just remind students that the events in the book are one year earlier than the date on the spine.

Anitra Gordon, Lincoln High School, Ypsilanti, Michigan
The Book Report • May/June 2000 (Volume 19, Issue 1)

Inexpensive Dry Erase Board

It is easy to make an inexpensive dry erase board. Purchase a sheet of shower lining from a building supply store. The sheets are large and a fraction of the cost of a dry erase board. You may want to have the sheet cut into several dry erase boards. The building supply store may be willing to cut it for you.

Debra Kay Logan, Mt. Gilead (Ohio) High School
Library Media Connection • April/May 2003 (Volume 21, Issue 7)

Thrifty Laminating

We often receive catalogs featuring timely library promotional materials that we cannot afford. We give these catalogs and scissors to students who are staying in from recess, because of detention or injuries, and to drop-in parent or student helpers and ask them to cut out the larger designs, mottoes, or pictures. A basketful of these designs is kept by the pouch laminator. Whenever a whole pouch is not being used, these "fillers" or rectangles of jazzy wrapping paper are tucked into spare spaces. This gives us crisp, free, laminated bookmarks with no copyright infringements.

Sheryl Kindle Fullner, Nooksack Valley Middle School, Everson, Washington
Library Media Connection • October 2003 (Volume 22, Issue 2)

Graphic Spirals

As the popularity of graphic novels increases, the bindings wear down and the pages fall out. A cheap way to increase the life of your graphic novels is to have them spiral-bound. This can be done at a local print shop or your school district's Print Services Department for about $1.50 per book—a small price to pay when you consider lengthening the life of the book by an extra year or so!

Laura Stiles, Cedar Valley Middle School, Austin, Texas
Library Media Connection • February 2006 (Volume 24, Issue 5)

A Magnetic Personality

Poetry magnets are intriguing, but the size is small and the cost is large. Whenever you visit a convention, trade show or fair, pick up every free magnet available. Cut the magnets into two or more strips depending on their size. Students or adults can type words (14–20 point size) in columns on a sheet of paper. Laminate the paper or cover each word with wide library tape, trim, and attach with spray adhesive to a magnet strip. Kids like nominating words for the magnets. Metal doorframes, cookie sheets, and teacher desk fronts are good playing fields for the poetry.

Sheryl Kindle Fullner, Nooksack Valley Middle School, Everson, Washington
Library Media Connection • February 2005 (Volume 23, Issue 5)

DISPLAYS

A Fishy Display Case

In our library media center we often display arts, crafts, and collections along with our books. Used upside down aquariums are crisp looking substitutes for expensive cases. They may often be purchased for less than five dollars at yard sales and thrift shops. They fit most standard library shelves and are easy to change by simply lifting one edge to insert new items.

Sheryl Kindle Fullner, Nooksack Valley Middle School, Everson, Washington
Library Media Connection • November/December 2003 (Volume 22, Issue 3)

They're Framed!

Buy several inexpensive 8" x 10" picture frames. Place framed pictures of famous people all over the library, and display books by or about the people featured.

Charlotte Allen, Craigmont High School, Memphis, Tennessee
Library Media Connection • January 2005 (Volume 23, Issue 4)

Cost-Cutting Showcases

I use solid-color, plastic tablecloths to cover the backgrounds of the library showcases. They're bigger than any paper I could buy, cheap ($2), and they don't tear.

Diane Alexander, Liberty High School, Brentwood, California
The Book Report • May/June 2002 (Volume 21, Issue 1)

Check Out Our Banners

Modern newspapers don't fit into those ancient wooden newspaper spindles efficiently, so we have turned our aged spindles into display rods for cloth or rip-stop nylon banners. We drilled a slanted hole into a small piece of 2" x 4", which was screwed into the wall near our entry. The banners are often on sale after holidays, but the "poles" or rods seldom are. The spindles are also great for hanging promotional T-shirts and ethnic clothing.

Sheryl Kindle Fullner, Nooksack Valley Middle School, Everson, Washington
Library Media Connection • February 2006 (Volume 24, Issue 5)

Balloon Mania

If you get a large mylar balloon for the library, use a straw to completely deflate it when finished, and store it flat with no wrinkles. Most local balloon purveyors will refill mylar for free or for less than a dollar. You can gradually build a library of balloons for all subjects. In your newsletter, encourage people to donate their mylar balloons. An eagle, Yoda, and a butterfly are our best ones so far.

Sheryl Kindle Fullner, Nooksack Valley Middle School, Everson, Washington
Library Media Connection • November/December 2004 (Volume 23, Issue 3)

Display Dilemma

No time to make a display this month? Ask your local video rental store for their free posters and 3-D display stands when they are done with them. You can cut up posters and take apart display stands to use just the parts you want.

Amy Johnston, Swift Current Comprehensive High School,
 Swift Current, SK, Canada
Library Media Connection • March 2004 (Volume 22, Issue 6)

Ethnic Decorations

Ethnic clothing is a great visual tie-in to library promotions. We have borrowed a sari, a hanbok, a kimono, a Mexican skirt and blouse, and a tribal button blanket to promote different holidays such as Cinco de Mayo and Lunar New Year as well as multi-cultural authors. To show garments off to best advantage, run a bamboo pole through the arms and use a ceiling suspension method. This way the display is not confined to a wall, but can be hung overhead anywhere in the library.

Sheryl Kindle Fullner, Nooksack Valley Middle School, Everson, Washington
Library Media Connection • October 2004 (Volume 23, Issue 2)

Dive into Books!

Last year, to promote my "Dive into Books!" spring reading program, I set up a fish tank next to the circulation desk. I bought live bearing Mollies, some orange and some black, to match our school's colors. The Mollies and their babies were a huge hit with the students! Instead of teasing and jostling each other while waiting to check out books, they watched the fish instead. Needless to say, I have decided to make the fish tank a permanent feature in my IMC.

Michelle Glatt, Chiddix Junior High School, Normal, Illinois
Library Media Connection • April/May 2005 (Volume 23, Issue 7)

Going Mobile

Make mobiles from your antique, broken, or out-of-date a/v media. We painted old movie reels to use for the base, and hung a few film strips and their colorful plastic cases, some out-of-date periodical CDs, and a few defunct floppy discs. The middle support wire is a computer mouse (minus its rotator ball)! The students think they are great... and we find them to be entertaining and creative works of art!

Carol Bassett & Cheri Hansen, Arlington High School Library, Arlington, Washington
Library Talk • March/April 2002 (Volume 15, Issue 2)

Throw in the Towel

Pricey teen posters promoting reading are sometimes dull photographs accompanied by captions such as "Rockin' Good Read." Instead of posters, our library purchases end-of-the-season beach towels, which are frequently marked down to about $7.00—far cheaper, more durable, and considerably flashier when suspended from a dowel attached to our ceiling hooks with monofilament fishing line. They store without creasing and make great reading incentive prizes. Large print captions on paper can be stapled to them with a long bindery stapler.

 Sheryl Kindle Fullner, Nooksack Valley Middle School, Everson, Washington
Library Media Connection • August/September 2004 (Volume 23, Issue 1)

Guys and Gals

Display titles side-by-side in an interesting way—"Chic picks" and "Guy Faves" make a hip and fun way to encourage selection. Put pictures or props of "girlie" or "macho" items in your display such as flowers, costume jewelry, and shopping bags for the ladies and toy trucks, playing cards, and sports equipment for the gents. Students enjoy seeing what their peers are reading, and teachers appreciate the suggestions when directing students to find a book for an assignment.

 Sharon L. Bush, West Genesee High School, Camillus, New York
Library Media Connection • March 2006 (Volume 24, Issue 6)

Pole Displays

In our LMC we use "barnacle" clips attached to our ceiling frets to suspend two loops of 24-inch clear monofilament fishing line. Through these loops we place a four-foot bamboo pole. This is used to support posters, etc. for library promotions. To reinforce different themes, we have substituted a red, white and blue dowel, a long golf club, a fishing rod, a broom, a mop, a long-handled butterfly net, a hoe, and a tree branch. The possibilities are endless.

 Sheryl Kindle Fullner, Nooksack Valley Middle School, Everson, Washington
Library Media Connection • October 2004 (Volume 23, Issue 2)

High Carb Reading

My book orders suddenly filled up with bread books, and not the recipe kind: *The Breadwinner; The Bread Winner; Burned Bread* and *Chutney; The Risen Bread; The Bread Loaf* (poetry anthology); *Only Bread, Only Light; Peace! Land! Bread!; Peace and Bread;* and *White Bread Competition,* etc. In the past to showcase depression era books on breadlines such as those from the Dear America series, I borrowed several automatic breadmakers and purchased breadmix on sale. The wafting aroma lured some non-library users into my clutches. Sometimes librarians neglect the sense of smell in promoting media. Think of it as an olfactory bulletin board.

Sheryl Fullner, Nooksack Valley Middle School, Everson, Washington
Library Media Connection • March 2006 (Volume 24, Issue 6)

Library Display Case Ideas

These suggestions may help you accent your library display cases:

> • For Poetry Month highlight "Popular and Peculiar Poetry."
>   Entice students to read various poems by eccentric poets,
>   such as Edward Lear, and answer questions for a library prize.
>
> • For the last month of school, feature your summer reading list
>   with "Barbie's Best Beach Books." Show Barbies in beach attire reading
>   and sitting on stacks of summer reading books.
>
> • At any time during the year display movie posters reflecting movie
>   ideas that originated from books. Possible display themes could
>   include "Have you Read Any Good Movies Lately?" or "Star Wars and
>   Beyond," with Star Wars memorabilia and books, for example.

Students will actually talk about the library displays!

L.M. Adriance, Washington Irving Middle School, Springfield, Virginia
The Book Report • March/April 2000 (Volume 18, Issue 5)

Clean Up Your Act, Clean Up Your World

If your library is often asked to feature student-created Ecology or Anti-Smoking, Anti-Drug posters, display these easily without making holes in your walls. String a clothesline from one side of the library to the other and hang the Clean Up posters with clothespins. Kids who have used dryers all their lives may be unfamiliar with fascinating pulley clotheslines. Retractable lines and pulley lines may be borrowed or purchased used. You can also use them to hang up photocopied pink and blue baby bloomers or baby pictures for school shower decorations. A hi-tech version of this (suitable for art) is available as a photo drying wire and clips.

Sheryl Kindle Fullner, Nooksack Valley Middle School, Everson, Washington
Library Media Connection • October 2004 (Volume 23, Issue 2)

Planning Ahead

During the last week of school I make a list of the books needed for the beginning of the next school year. I then play a game and have the students locate the books and pull them from the shelves. I clean them and have a nice display ready for the first staff meeting.

Cheryl Hartman, Dr. John Hole School, Centerville, Ohio
Library Media Connection • April/May 2005 (Volume 23, Issue 7)

Celebrate Dewey!

Tired of dragging out the same sets of books for various holidays and curriculum emphases? Try using the ten major divisions of Dewey: one for each month of the school year beginning with 000 and ending with 999. A local dollar store may have some very large modern metal stand up frames. Using fancy fonts, fill each of three frames with info on the Dewey number of the month. The whole nine months' worth of fillers will be stored in each frame. Simply swap out the info with a fresh page from the back of the frame each month. Decorate the LMC door with a giant 100's or 200's, etc. cut out of bright repositionable contact paper.

Sheryl Kindle Fullner, Nooksack Valley Middle School, Everson, Washington
Library Media Connection • November/December 2004 (Volume 23, Issue 3)

BULLETIN
BOARDS

Perpetual Library Bulletin Board

Set up a perpetual library bulletin board titled "Good News at My School" (substitute your school's name), and use it to feature newspaper clippings about students. Depending upon your locale and the time of year, the good-news board may feature sports, literary and community events, or other kinds of positive news about students. Give student library aides or helpers responsibility for cutting out or photocopying newspaper articles and periodically updating the board. This project contributes to a supportive, student-centered library environment, recognizes student achievements, encourages students to read, reinforces the analytical skills of the student library aides or helpers, takes care of the bulletin board, and makes you look good.

Sherry York, Ruidoso, New Mexico
Library Media Connection • January 2003 (Volume 21, Issue 4)

"Students & Teachers in the News" Bulletin Board

An easy, effective way to recognize your teachers and students who make the news in your hometown newspapers is to have a "Students & Teachers in the News" bulletin board. Cut out the articles and pictures and display them proudly on this board in the library media center. This has proven to be a popular attraction in our LMC!

Judean A. Unmuth-Shelley, Woodworth Middle School, Fond du Lac, Wisconsin
Library Media Connection • January 2005 (Volume 23, Issue 4)

Organizing Bulletin Board Materials

To keep bulletin board materials organized, make a picture of the finished bulletin board (or use the picture from which the idea came), and store this along with the caption letters and any pieces small enough to place in a 9" x 12" envelope. On the outside of the envelope, I write the caption and date it was used. Store large pieces in large cabinet drawers with the pieces paper-clipped together and the caption written on an index card, which is also clipped onto the pieces. Then arrange the envelopes in a filing cabinet drawer behind the following headings: Books, Christmas, Easter, Fall, February, Halloween, Library, March, May, Miscellaneous, New Year's, Reading, September, Special, and Thanksgiving. Most everything fits under these headings. Behind each heading, file the envelopes in alphabetical order according to the caption written on the envelope. When a new bulletin board is needed, simply look under the appropriate heading, pull out the envelope, locate the larger pieces, and assemble the board.

 Dorothy Pope, Lawrence County High School, Lawrenceburg, Tennessee
Library Media Connection • February 2006 (Volume 24, Issue 5)

Other Uses for Book Jackets

So many new books now come with book jackets that have exactly the same information and illustrations printed on the front covers. Especially in junior and senior high, it is not always necessary to keep and attach a mylar jacket on a well-made book. Instead, process those books without their jackets and use the jackets for bulletin boards and other displays. You can staple the jackets on a bulletin board of "New Items" or a theme you have created. Students can see the jackets on display and then check out the book(s) that caught their interest.

 Trisha Lake, Elk Island Public Schools, Sherwood Park, Alberta, Canada
Library Media Connection • January 2006 (Volume 24, Issue 4)

Tissue Paper Border

Tissue paper makes an inexpensive border for a bulletin board. Simply crinkle up the paper lengthwise and staple it to the board. The wide selection of colors and designs adds uniqueness, as well as a 3-D effect. A black background with a cream-colored tissue paper border is a classy way to display student artwork. Use brightly colored tissue paper to add a splash of color.

Julie Handyside, Faith Bible High School, Hillsboro, Oregon
Library Media Connection • February 2006 (Volume 24, Issue 5)

A Poet Tree in the Library

No bulletin board has attracted so many visitors as our large paper tree whose branches were filled with student written poems. Poetry writing was the classroom activity of an English teacher who was thrilled that we highlighted her students' work. Of course, the students enjoyed sharing their efforts school wide. The state poet laureate who had evaluated their work came and awarded the local prizes in front of the library's Poet Tree.

Connie Quirk, G. S. Mickelson Middle School, Brookings, South Dakota
Library Media Connection • March 2006 (Volume 24, Issue 6)

Mesmerizing Bulletin Board

We have a high interest bulletin board aimed at students ages 11 to 18. When some major long-term event hits the news and generates dozens of political cartoons, we post those on a low bulletin board at reading height. These cartoons are available within copyright laws from the Internet and only take a few minutes to print out five or six at a time. Occasionally the library offers a candy bar for the first person who can answer a trivia question about the cartoons. Winners' names are posted.

Sheryl Kindle Fullner, Nooksack Valley Middle School, Everson, Washington
Library Media Connection • March 2004 (Volume 22, Issue 6)

WORKING
WITH STUDENTS IN THE
LIBRARY

Students come to the library for a variety of reasons including, but not limited to, checking out books, checking out the area, and checking to see who is there. They come to take tests, to do make-up work, and occasionally to research and to read. Sometimes they are in the library because they wish to be and sometimes because they have to be. Once in a while, they come to return overdue books! Regardless of their motivations or their behavior patterns, we welcome these teens—potential readers and researchers and the reason for our being.

Tips in this section involve:

- Students
- Overdue Books

STUDENTS

Rules, Rules, Rules

The first few days of a school year are filled with rules, rules, and more rules. By the time I see students the second or third day of school, they are rule experts. Instead of telling students the rules, have them tell them to you. A well placed question here and there will fill in any rules they miss. When students suggest a rule, indicate any consequences.

Debra Kay Logan, Mt. Gilead (Ohio) High School
Library Media Connection • April/May 2004 (Volume 22, Issue 7)

Library Noise @ Lunch

With over 2,200 students at our school, lunch was a zoo my first year. Now we have a "No Problem!" lunchtime by creating zones for different activities. As they enter, those wanting to read current periodicals slip into an easy chair with a newspaper or magazine. To their right is a zone for the sociable crowd where the "lunch bunch" talks, tutors, plays chess, or exchanges ideas with friends. In this zone, noise is not an issue; it's okay. To the left of the reading area is a zone filled with computers, electronic resources, the Internet, and a typing area. These folks are so engrossed with computers, it is relatively quiet. Beside this area is a quiet zone where students can do serious research, study, and homework without distractions. After a few weeks of directions, the young people gravitate to the area they need. We make everyone happy from the chatterboxes to the studious.

Gay Ann Loesch, Independence High School, Charlotte, North Carolina
The Book Report • November/December 2000 (Volume 19, Issue 3)

Library Pass

I request that students stop by the library and get a lunch time pass when they want to visit the library after lunch. That way, I know how many students to expect, and the library doesn't become an extension of the cafeteria.

 Arlene Kachka, Luther High School, North Chicago, Illinois
The Book Report • May/June 2000 (Volume 19, Issue 1)

Chaos Reduction Theory

Students who wish to visit the library at lunchtime sign in on a sheet that includes their name and the purpose for the visit. Students who leave may re-enter with permission only. Those who truly want to take advantage of the library's collection and services appreciate this policy. They can read, work, or browse without being disturbed by groups wandering in to "check out the scene," socialize, or cause disturbances. We now spend less time supervising and more time assisting.

 Vickie Rabourn, Los Osos (California) Middle School
The Book Report • January/February 2002 (Volume 20, Issue 4)

Quiet Test Time Fillers

The library is one of our state testing sites. I purchase jigsaw puzzles with an educational theme such as the American Revolution and lay the pieces out on a table. When students are finished testing, but are waiting for others to get finished before they can start a new test section, they can work on the puzzle. I also bring in chess sets. Students can do both activities quietly. I have a big bunch of "regulars" that hang out in the morning. They enjoy playing chess and working the puzzles as well.

 Karen Boyle, Lloyd Memorial High School, Erlanger, Kentucky
Library Media Connection • April/May 2006 (Volume 24, Issue 7)

Tests/Makeup Work Folders

Keep a two-pocket folder for each teacher. Tests or makeup work to be done in the library go in the left-hand pocket with the students' names on them. Completed work goes in the right-hand pocket. Place the folders in a simple open file, such as an "in" box. Teachers come in daily to check their folders for completed work and to add new items.

Anne Shipley, Waterloo, New York
The Book Report • September/October 2000 (Volume 19, Issue 2)

Passage to Field Trips

To keep track of students on a field trip, laminate a small number of "Field Trip Passes." To keep track of trips to the concession stand and the restroom, students who are old enough to leave the main activity with a buddy get a pass but MUST stay together. Each pass gone represented a group of 2-3 students. With a limited number of passes to distribute you have a better idea of how many are gone. When a pass comes back, another group of 2-3 can leave. You can easily identify students from your group by the passes they carry.

Janice Gumerman, Bingham Seventh Grade Center, Independence, Missouri
Library Media Connection • November/December 2003 (Volume 22, Issue 3)

Make-up Tests

If you proctor make-up tests and quizzes in your library media center, get two letter trays for your workroom. One will have folders for different subjects or specific teachers. The teachers bring the tests and quizzes, with the students' names on them, into the library media center and put them in the appropriate folder. The teachers must also write the student a pass to get out of study hall to come take the test or quiz. Put the students at various individual desks reserved for test takers. When the quizzes or tests are completed, put them in a second tray for the teachers to pick up.

Teresa Higus, Morton (Illinois) High School
Library Media Connection • October 2005 (Volume 24, Issue 2)

No Blame Game

To avoid "blame" type arguments, I use one magic phrase: "I am sure you did not do it, but could you fix it for me?" This applies to the group of guys with a purple pen sitting next to purple graffiti. It applies to the kid that I saw tossing the book up in the air and bringing it back with a torn cover. It works for helter-skelter chairs, litter, and encyclopedias shelved upside down. No arguments about who did it. Just the necessity that someone be accountable for fixing it. No tool is fool proof, but this one has a high rate of success. Since it is not accompanied by an accusation, most kids seem to see this as "fair."

Sheryl Kindle Fullner, Nooksack Valley Middle School, Everson, Washington
Library Media Connection • April/May 2004 (Volume 22, Issue 7)

Questions for Bookmarks

Our library, like most middle school libraries, was giving away lots of bookmarks. However, I noticed that many of them were forgotten in books, left lying around the library, or were sometimes destroyed. Because we were freely dispensing them and it seemed as though they were not appreciated, we decided to start charging for them. But we don't take cash; we give them out to students who are willing to answer questions about the library. Most students love the challenge, and we always give a bookmark, whether or not they know the answer. If they don't know the answer, we prompt them or have them go around the library and find the answer. We ask questions such as "What is a biography?" "Where are the biographies?" "What is a call number?" and "In which Dewey section are the books about sports?" We have many more questions, and we try to match the question with the ability of the student. But we always make sure a student understands the answer and gets a bookmark as well. It's an enjoyable way for the students to learn about the library or reinforce what they already know. Some students come in begging for a question!

Renee Mick, Franco Middle School, Presidio, Texas
Library Media Connection • April/May 2004 (Volume 22, Issue 7)

Freebie Fun

Collect all the freebies that you get from various jobbers throughout the year. Some companies send things such as calculators, radios, or CD players when you buy a certain amount of merchandise. Often Book Fairs award free soft-cover books to the library media specialists as a promotional device. Use these freebies to give out as contest prizes throughout the year. Students appreciate the special recognition and the cool prizes.

Ann M. G. Gray, Pittsburg (New Hampshire) School
Library Media Connection • February 2006 (Volume 24, Issue 5)

Students are Card-Carrying Members

To help our middle school students to be responsible for their own library patron cards, we give each child a plastic, self-sealing snack bag and tape it to a common page in their agenda book during orientation. Because the agenda is used as their pass, students always carry their cards!

Carolyn Oakley, Henrico County Public Schools, Richmond, Virginia
The Book Report • September/October 2001 (Volume 20, Issue 2)

Juvenile Offenders in the LMC

If there are local, non-violent teens who need to work off community service hours, they can be a great library asset. They may excel at moving hundreds of books or re-labeling many hundreds more if any type of conversion is going on such as attaching security tapes. Three caveats: lock your purse/wallet/or briefcase in your trunk along with any logs of passwords and user names. Do not leave the worker unsupervised in the LMC even if you as Librarian need to use the restroom or drinking fountain. Create an upbeat, appreciative, no-nonsense environment from day one. Reward the worker with a choice from among several teen paperbacks that are new looking, a graphic novel, or food.

Sheryl Kindle Fullner, Nooksack Valley Middle School, Everson, Washington
Library Media Connection • August/September 2004 (Volume 23, Issue 1)

OVERDUE BOOKS

Getting the Message Out about Overdue Books

Like most school librarians, I have trouble getting some of my high school students to return overdue library materials. For long-overdues, I call the students down to the library and ask if they have an answering machine at home. Most students do, so I have them call home and leave themselves a message to return the library materials. It works better than a letter to parents, and most students have fun talking to themselves on the machine.

 Christine Nowicki, Montoursville (Pennsylvania) Area High School
The Book Report • May/June 2002 (Volume 21, Issue 1)

Overdue Lists

When sending out a list of students with overdue material within a specific classroom, I ask teachers to have students initial their names on the list and return the list to my box. I then put all the classroom lists in a binder. This helps to verify that students have been notified. On this first level of notification, before the individual notes go out, it helps to avoid excuses such as "my teacher never told me" or "I never saw my name on any list." Our school's discipline is based on documenting the number of contacts with the student. (It also alerts me as to which teachers actually do fall into the "never told me" category.)

 Sheryl Kindle Fullner, Nooksack Valley Middle School, Everson, Washington
Library Media Connection • March 2005 (Volume 23, Issue 6)

Promptness Pays

To encourage students to bring back their books on time, start a promotion for the "10,000th Checkout" in your library media center. At the start of school, set the circulation counter to zero and watch the checkout number increase daily. When it approaches 9,800 checkouts, make a morning announcement stating that whoever checks out the 10,000th book will win a bag full of prizes. Remind the students to bring their books back on time so that they may be the 10,000th checkout. When you have a winner, ring a bell and give the student prizes such as books, pencils, bookmarks, and other freebies that you pick up at conventions. At the end-of-day announcements, read the winner's name, along with the list of prizes. Then remind students to keep on returning their books on time so that they may be the lucky winner of the 20,000th Checkout.

Esther Peck, Wemrock Brook School, Manalapan, New Jersey
Library Media Connection • January 2005 (Volume 23, Issue 4)

Positive End to the Year

I always struggle to get overdue library books back and fines paid at the end of the school year, and decided a positive approach is best. I print out a list of students, buy a BIG batch of mini candy bars (all kinds), then announce for students to stop by and check if their media account is all clear. It is amazing how cheerfully students pay fines to get that one piece of candy! Almost all student accounts are clear by the time school is out. The cost of the candy is no more than one lost book. It is good PR also, as it gives me a chance to wish them a good summer. Next year I hope to have a classy flier of suggested books to read over the summer to give them with their candy.

Donna Wenzel, La Vista (Nebraska) Junior High
Library Media Connection • April/May 2005 (Volume 23, Issue 7)

Finding Overdue Books

At the end of the year, on locker cleanout day, stalk the hallways with overdue list in hand and seek out the offenders. You can get all your overdue books back and even some that escaped the checkout.

 Victoria Blaser, Tiverton (Rhode Island) High School
Library Media Connection • April/May 2004 (Volume 22, Issue 7)

Year-End Fines

If you have problems collecting fines at the end of the school, purchase a boxful of candy from the local dollar store. For every patron who has no fines or overdue books when they turn in all their books, allow them to choose a piece of candy from the candy box. Many will pay for fines and lost books just to get a penny piece of candy in front of their peers.

 Julia Phillips, Ashville (Alabama) Middle School
Library Media Connection • April/May 2006 (Volume 24, Issue 7)

TEACHING
RESEARCH
SKILLS

Middle and secondary school students may have the basic skills for conducting research in the library but can usually benefit from help in refining those skills so that time spent researching in the library is productive and on-target. In the ideal situation, students become familiar with the school library and are familiar with that environment before they begin an actual research project.

Teachers and school librarians work together to make the research experience a positive learning experience that encourages higher-level thinking to produce a product, perhaps a written paper or presentation that can communicate new knowledge—a far cry from the dreaded research paper of years past. Twenty-first century librarians are ready and willing to help students utilize all library resources to obtain information. Replaced by the Internet, not!

Tips in this section include:

- Library Orientation
- Before a Research Project
- During a Research Project
- After a Research Project

LIBRARY
ORIENTATION

Scavenger Hunt Contest

When orienting new freshmen to the library media center, I hold a scavenger hunt where students are each given a form with different book categories (fiction, nonfiction, new books, or career). After finding an example of each, they also answer questions about key library media center rules that I want to reinforce. When each student finishes with the form, he or she brings it to me, and I check it on the spot. The first ten completely correct forms go into a basket, and we draw one winner who receives a "goody bag" with small school items (floppy disk, pencil, and highlighter) along with a candy bar. Almost every student is motivated to participate in order to win!

 Tish Carpinelli, Lower Cape May (New Jersey) Regional High School
Library Media Connection • August/September 2005 (Volume 24, Issue 1)

T-Shirt Team Names

Doing a cooperative learning activity in the library media center? Base team names on whatever t-shirts students happen to be wearing that day. Say, "This is the Buckeye team. This is the Blue Jacket team…" The class will figure out how they are being named by the time the last group is being named.

 Debra Kay Logan, Mt. Gilead (Ohio) High School
Library Media Connection • April/May 2003 (Volume 21, Issue 7)

Introducing Interlibrary Loan

To demonstrate how specialized and informed an expert can be, I show an assortment of specialized professional journals. I have a collection of potato growing journals. The students love titles such as *The Badger Common Tater, American Journal of Potato Research, Potato Grower, Potato Country,* and *The Great Lakes Fruit and Vegetable Growers News.* I always save the best for last—*Spud Man.* After the shock wears off and the laughter dies down, we consider the possibility of resources like this being available in local libraries. The consensus is that even the local university is unlikely to have any of them on hand. This is a good time to remind students about interlibrary loan. Ask the students if a person who reads these types of materials might be more up-to-date and informed than if he or she had used other resources. They invariably say yes!

Debra Kay Logan, Mt. Gilead (Ohio) High School
Library Media Connection • March 2003 (Volume 21, Issue 6)

Resource Speeches vs. Worksheet

Our students always started their speech and research classes with a scavenger hunt to find all their resource areas in the media centers. It was not one of their happiest assignments. For a change, we planned a new strategy: Their first speeches' topics would be "these specific resources and how to use them." Each student presented a resource and told how it is used. This approach gave the students an easy first speech. Materials were readily available; they didn't have to do the dreaded scavenger hunt. A short hands-on quiz followed to assess what every student learned. Students said they enjoyed the change.

Jane Cabaya, Century High School, Rochester, Minnesota
Library Media Connection • February 2003 (Volume 21, Issue 5)

Rap It Up

This rap has helped our students memorize the association between call number and spine label. We use the couplets in a lesson on spotting call numbers. The students draw out the words call and spine as they say the rap.

"These are the facts.

I'll lay them on the table.

Memorize them to the max.

I know that you are able.

The c-a-l-l number's

on the s-p-i-n-e label.

The c-a-l-l number's

on the s-p-i-n-e label."

Sheryl Kindle Fullner, Nooksack Valley Middle School, Everson, Washington
Library Media Connection • February 2004 (Volume 22, Issue 5)

BEFORE
A RESEARCH PROJECT

Research Process Guide

At the beginning of the year, photocopy a packet of materials that you create on the research process. Organize the guides around your research philosophy or process, and mesh them with the way you will teach research in the library. Include different worksheets designed for each part of the process. If teachers come into the library to sign up for research time, but didn't have time to plan with you, offer them a copy of the packet. Both new teachers and experienced ones will be happy to have the packet as they plan their unit.

Carolyn Foote, Westlake High School Library, Austin, Texas
Library Media Connection • January 2004 (Volume 22, Issue 4)

Peer Teaching Produces A+ Results

During a recent library visit to find information for biology projects, ninth and 10th grade students had the opportunity to participate in a peer teaching activity. Before students arrived, we prepared activity sheets for each of the library's online, subscription databases. The sheets listed a series of tasks to practice, using suggested "successful" search terms, and were designed to highlight the special strength of each database.

Students worked in groups of two or three and practiced the search tasks on their assigned database for about 10 minutes. The groups then demonstrated the basic use of each database while "broadcasting" their searches from the teaching station to the rest of the class. Students were actively engaged in the process and enjoyed their teaching experiences, while learning about the databases from each other.

Sandy McLuckie, Episcopal High School Library, Jacksonville, Florida
The Book Report • May/June 2002 (Volume 21, Issue 1)

Hunting for Citations

The concept of bibliographic citation can be difficult for students to understand. Try a reverse approach when introducing bibliographic formats so that students can experience firsthand the importance of correct, exact publication information. Hold a scavenger hunt. Hand out bibliographic citations to students and have them find treasures in a variety of resource materials (books, online or print encyclopedias, magazines, online databases, Web sites, or CD-ROMs).

Mary C. Jones, Eagleview Middle School, Colorado Springs, Colorado
Library Media Connection • February 2006 (Volume 24, Issue 5)

Citation Cheat Sheet

Students always ask how to cite a particular source in MLA format, especially electronic databases and Internet sources. I printed pages for all the available print and non-print sources available to students in our school library. This way I can hand the students a sheet with an example of how the source is cited in MLA format or the whole six-page packet of MLA source citations. This saves time and gives the students a hands-on reference sheet, which can be kept in their notebooks.

Ellen Speirs, Cheshire (Connecticut) High School
Library Media Connection • April/May 2004 (Volume 22, Issue 7)

Visuals and Displays

When discussing an activity or project with students, use as many visuals as possible and display sample projects. Show examples from past years or create samples for display.

Debra Kay Logan, Mt. Gilead (Ohio) High School
Library Media Connection • November/December 2003 (Volume 22, Issue 3)

Finding Keywords

If research time is limited for a project, make that a consideration when selecting links for online research. Is the information readily available? Is the site searchable? Also, teach students how to use the Find feature of their browser. Simultaneously pressing the Control key (open apple key on a Mac) and the "F" key will open a Find box on many browsers. This will allow the searcher to quickly locate keywords in a Web site.

Debra Kay Logan, Mt. Gilead (Ohio) High School
Library Media Connection • April/May 2004 (Volume 22, Issue 7)

Pre-Project Presentation

In our high school library, we felt as though we were giving the same pre-project presentation over and over again: how and where to find relevant books, what references would apply, what Internet sources might help, and so forth. So we created a series of specialized handouts that provide starting points for our students on the most common research assignments we see: careers, current or controversial issues, biographies, authors and literary criticism, and 20th-century decades. A supply of these sheets is kept in a slotted display box at the end of the circulation counter, and the texts are also posted on our Web site (**www.u46.k12.il.us/ehs/library/how.htm**). Now whenever a class comes to the library to do research on those topics, we distribute the appropriate handouts to everyone, including the teacher, and give an abbreviated speech highlighting the essentials. We know that some students are actually listening to us and reading along with us. But if they're not, or if some of them arrive late on the scene, they'll always have the printed page to refer to.

Corinne H. Smith, Elgin (Illinois) High School
The Book Report • November/December 2002 (Volume 21, Issue 3)

Sample Presentation Notes

Working with students who have to give an oral presentation? Make transparencies or a PowerPoint display of presentation note cards to show students the type of notes that should be used in their presentations.

Debra Kay Logan, Mt. Gilead (Ohio) High School
Library Media Connection • January 2003 (Volume 21, Issue 4)

Cheating: A Tip For You

Create a link from your media center homepage to your district Internet Safety and Responsible Use Policy. Also create a PowerPoint presentation on copyright. Educate the staff about some of the tools available to ensure responsible actions by students when using the Internet for research. Encourage teachers to use a research template for note taking that allows students to cut and paste valuable information from Internet sites. However, they must also complete the bibliographic information on the template as well as provide original ideas and fresh insight. You might wish to subscribe to a service such as <**Turnitin.com**>. You may not completely rid your school community of the "cheating beast," but you can get the message out that it is not acceptable and will not be tolerated.

Julie Perry, Croatan High School, Newport, North Carolina
Library Media Connection • November/December 2003 (Volume 22, Issue 3)

Introducing Storyboarding

Introduce storyboarding by asking students if they have ever watched a cooking show and thought about the planning involved. Invariably there are comments about the food being cooked in advance, pre-measured ingredients, and the supplies that are waiting just under the counter. Talk about the planning involved.

Debra Kay Logan, Mt. Gilead (Ohio) High School
Library Media Connection • February 2003 (Volume 21, Issue 5)

DURING
A RESEARCH PROJECT

Journaling During Research

Make journaling a part of major research projects. Each time students stop working, have them write down a couple of sentences about what they have accomplished. Suggest that they include the date, places searched, decisions made, needed information, and interesting discoveries. Also, have them write notes about what they want to do next.

Debra Kay Logan, Mt. Gilead (Ohio) High School
Library Media Connection • March 2005 (Volume 23, Issue 6)

Bibliographic Cheat Sheet

Laminate a "cheat sheet" of the basic bibliography formats. Make them brightly colored and easy to find, or leave them next to computers for quick reference. Kids will come to depend on them.

Kathy Fritts, Jesuit High School, Portland, Oregon
The Book Report • March/April 2001 (Volume 19, Issue 5)

Scanning for Facts

When students are looking for numerical information like height or weight, point out that skimming and scanning can help them find number facts quickly and easily. Remind them that they still need to read to know what they have actually found.

Debra Kay Logan, Mt. Gilead (Ohio) High School
Library Media Connection • August/September 2003 (Volume 22, Issue 1)

Use Manila Folders for Organization

During a major project planning session, give (or sell for a nickel) each student a manila file folder for his or her project. Make a stapler or paper clips available for students to attach critical papers. The folder impresses upon students that it is important that they keep track of their notes and other papers.

Debra Kay Logan, Mt. Gilead (Ohio) High School
Library Media Connection • October 2003 (Volume 22, Issue 2)

Organizing Notes

If a student is having a hard time organizing their notes for a written report or oral presentation, help them determine the different aspects of their topic. Next have them use different colored highlighters to identify and group the topic aspects before they start writing. When they write they should pull the color-coded like items together.

Debra Kay Logan, Mt. Gilead (Ohio) High School
Library Media Connection • February 2003 (Volume 21, Issue 5)

No Child Left Without a Reference Librarian. . .

Not every student writing a research paper consults the librarian to obtain help in finding information on a topic, yet sometimes the librarian may know the perfect database, ideal new book, or authoritative reference (volume that may be an invaluable resource). How can a high school librarian extend his or her reach to ALL students? This year, our Research and Composition teacher asked each student to enter his or her name, topic/thesis, and email address into a Word document. The teacher then emailed the document to me. When I opened the file, I had hotlinks to each student's email along with a description of his or her research question. The students were thrilled to get an email from the librarian with suggestions for sources and search strategies just for their project.

Mary Wepking, Central High School, Brookfield, Wisconsin
Library Media Connection • November/December 2005 (Volume 24, Issue 3)

AFTER
A RESEARCH PROJECT

Checking Student Sources

To check student sources for research papers, after the papers are turned in and graded, ask the teacher to bring the students with their papers back to the library. Hand back their papers and tell them to look at the end notes page, where you or the teacher will have circled specific references you would like to check, for instance, numbers 2, 4, 5, and 7. Request that the students produce those items for your and the teacher'ss inspection.

The kids will scramble to relocate what they had used. The library staff will scramble to get the back periodical issues out of the storage room for them and help them retrace their steps. As each student locates his or her sources, the teacher inspects the bibliographic form in the end notes or bibliography and checks the body of the paper to see if each was properly quoted or paraphrased. (You could also volunteer to check bibliographic form and let the teacher check the body of the paper.) This process short-circuits student-fabricated sources and dates and uncovers many direct quotes without proper credit.

You can do this in one period with a class of up to 30 students. For classes over 40, you will need about two class periods. If time is a constraint, you may wish to require copies of source materials, especially those from Internet resources.

Lee D. Gordon, Sierra Vista High School, Las Vegas, Nevada
Library Media Connection • February 2003 (Volume 21, Issue 5)

Research Survey

After the junior class research assignment, students fill out a survey rating the resources they used. I list all the online databases I showed them before they began their research. I ask them to indicate if they used resources from the Web, print resources from the library media center, or resources from other libraries. This identifies what resources were most valuable and assists in making budget decisions for the next school year. I also ask them if they have any "words of wisdom" to share with students who will do the research assignment next year.

Julie Burwinkel, Ursuline Academy, Cincinnati, Ohio
Library Media Connection • January 2006 (Volume 24, Issue 4)

COLLABORATING
WITH
TEACHERS

Secondary school librarians facilitate collaboration with teachers in a multitude of ways. They scheme to attract teachers to the library, frequently offering food and fun as lures. The librarian continually promotes library materials in a variety of creative ways. Always aware that the library collection must be relevant to the curricula of the school, the school librarian obtains input from teachers in as many subjects as possible. Librarians work with teachers in planning library activities that incorporate library use and research skills into meaningful lessons.

Tips in this section include:

- Attracting Teachers to the Library
- Promoting Library Materials
- Obtaining Input from Teachers
- Working Together
- Integrating Curricula

ATTRACTING
TEACHERS TO THE LIBRARY

Spread the Word

Need to spread the word and get your coworkers' attention? Post staff messages over the school's photocopier machine(s), on the wall behind shared phones, in the bathroom, or by teacher's mailboxes. If you have a flexible schedule, these locations are also effective places to post a copy of your schedule.

Deb Logan, Taft Middle School, Marion, Ohio
The Book Report • September/October 2000 (Volume 19, Issue 2)

Meet the New Books Party

Introduce your new books each year (and promote the library) with a staff "Tea and Chocolate" after school near the beginning of the year. Divide all the new books into subject areas and display them invitingly. Then have a goodies table with a fancy punch and platters of fruit and rich chocolate. The teachers will be impressed that you fussed so much for them—and that you are buying for their specific curricula!

Ellen Bell, Amador Valley High School, Pleasanton, California
Library Talk • May/June 2002 (Volume 15, Issue 3)

Forming Collaborative Partnerships

Looking for ways to form collaborative partnerships? Make markers, colored pencils, glue, scissors, and other materials available in the library media center. Invite teachers to use the library media center for researching and creating projects. Library tables are great work surfaces, especially for group projects.

Debra Kay Logan, Mt. Gilead (Ohio) High School
Library Media Connection • February 2003 (Volume 21, Issue 5)

Care Packages for New Teachers

Give new teachers a care package, containing library information sheets, a school map, the faculty list, and any other helpful information, at the start of the school year. Include some "treats"—a small pad of sticky notes, a fancy paper clip, a roll of Lifesavers candy, and/or some chocolate kisses and hugs—in a zipper-seal snack bag and staple it to the info sheets.

Debra Kay Logan, Mt. Gilead (Ohio) High School
Library Media Connection • April/May 2003 (Volume 21, Issue 7)

Sweet Treats

Take advantage of any holiday that is candy-related (Halloween, Christmas, Valentine's Day, St. Patrick's Day, Easter) to give faculty and staff candy bars in their mailboxes. Attach a label to each candy bar with the address and a Web site that you want teachers to look at. An online database site that you want students to use for research is a good start. Teachers love to receive the candy, and the label is a good way to remind them of a Web site to check out!

Ruth Riley, Poland (Ohio) Seminary High School
Library Media Connection • January 2005 (Volume 23, Issue 4)

Two Minutes of Technology

Teachers can be reluctant technology users and notoriously leery of change. We break this ice with "Two Minutes of Technology" at every faculty meeting, in which various teachers from different departments demonstrate a technology they're using. These presentations are brief, entertaining, real, and reassuring. On the agenda they're listed as "Brought to You by the Library," which gives us extra credibility, yet the only things we have to do are arrange for the presenters and introduce them.

Kathy Fritts, Jesuit High School, Portland, Oregon
The Book Report • September/October 2002 (Volume 21, Issue 2)

PROMOTING
LIBRARY MATERIALS

Promoting New Materials

Showcasing new materials is a priority to get students, faculty, and administrators to check them out. Each month, select at least three teachers to sample new library resources (a combination of books, videos, and CDs) and give you written or oral feedback on these items. Then make up a display with the teachers' school pictures along with their reviews. Students and other teachers love to see what teachers are reading and can't wait to check out the new items.

Mercedes Smith, Bishop Kenny High School, Jacksonville, Florida
The Book Report • September/October 2001 (Volume 20, Issue 2)

"Preview Packs" of New Titles

If you're finding your busy teachers don't read your newsletters filled with new titles and media information or come to see the latest display of new books, why not take the new titles to them? Our teachers like receiving "Preview Packs" of new books as they come in. We select books fitting their courses and interests and check them out for them. A media assistant hand delivers them to each teacher. Also, by going to classrooms, reading and booktalking new books, we entice the students to come see what's new at the media center. So, if your teachers and students won't come to you, go to them!

Gay Ann Loesch, Independence High School, Charlotte, North Carolina
The Book Report • November/December 2000 (Volume 19, Issue 3)

Special Lunch Displays

If your school has special lunches for faculty (birthday lunch, holiday potluck, etc.), you have a terrific opportunity to display new library materials. For a recent lunch, I sent invitations to faculty members asking them to come to a "book preview." The preview time started 15 minutes before the special lunch and ended 15 minutes after. Books and videos were displayed on tables in a supply room across from the faculty lounge. The proximity of the display area to the luncheon was a key component of the preview. Teachers were able to browse (and check out) the new books at their leisure. This preview time was more successful than others held before/during faculty meetings.

Laura D'Amato, Lake Ridge Academy, North Ridgeville, Ohio
Library Media Connection • February 2003 (Volume 21, Issue 5)

PUNderful Lists!

Our teachers love contests—especially when chocolate is involved! When our library receives new books, we type up a list: call number, author, title, and distribute it to our staff. To encourage them to look thru the list we put one fake title on each page. The teacher who finds all the fake titles first wins a large candy bar. Sample titles we have used: *The History of Moving Pictures* by Anna Mation. *Rapid Wealth in a Financially Uncertain World* by Robin Banks, etc.

Deborah Dick and Deborah Davis, Kickapoo High School, Springfield, Missouri
Library Media Connection • March 2005 (Volume 23, Issue 6)

Compliments of . . .

Make a rubber stamp entitled Compliments of (Fill in your media center name.). Each time you find an article, poster, magazine issue, etc. that you want to pass along to a colleague, rubber stamp a post-it onto the cover and put it in his or her box. This way he or she remembers who passed along the goodies!

Barbara Schiefler, Alvarado Middle School Media Center, Union City, California
Library Media Connection • October 2003 (Volume 22, Issue 2)

Connecting Kids and Library Resources

Do you have good fiction and nonfiction books that sit on your shelves, unnoticed? Select one teacher from each department and ask her for display space in her classroom. Hang book jackets on the teachers' bulletin boards or put the books in their window cases. Put math books in the math rooms, art and music titles in the fine arts rooms. Busy teachers will rejoice that you're taking over one of their many tasks, and most will gladly send a student to the library to check out the materials for display. Students and teachers will see what resources that support their projects and assignments are available in the library.

Dr. R. J. (Becky) Pasco, College of Education, University of Nebraska at Omaha
The Book Report • May/June 2002 (Volume 21, Issue 1)

Library Research Tidbits

When sending out communications, such as new book lists to teachers, I put a small blurb at the bottom that describes current school library research findings. This helps to promote the use of the library in the teaching and learning process among classroom teachers. [For example, one item might read: "Current research findings have revealed that student academic achievement is increased when collaborative planning between the classroom teacher and the school librarian occurs."]

Patricia L. Kolencik, North Clarion High School Library, Tionesta, Pennsylvania
The Book Report • March/April 2001 (Volume 19, Issue 5)

Books, Bagels, and Brand New Things

To promote awareness of the many new resources in the media center, I organized a "Books, Bagels, and Brand New Things Fest" in the media center just before Valentine's Day. I gathered all the new books we received in the media center during the last two grading periods and arranged them in categories on the media center tables. Additionally, I pulled out the latest copy of each periodical that we subscribe to in print and randomly scattered them on the media center tables. All new videos were pulled out and set out on the carts of three different mobile TV/VCR units. The media center was decorated in a Valentines theme with red tablecloths on each table and red and white paper hearts scattered on top. All of these new materials were arranged in a thematic fashion, with science type items together, fictional choices together, and so on. I composed a flyer in e-mail and hard copy inviting all staff members and administrators to the event. I served orange juice, teas, flavored coffee, and bagels with a variety of cream cheeses. The bagel feast started at 6:45 A.M. and continued into the middle of the day. Teachers came in to socialize, have a simple breakfast, and browse the new items in the media center. The response was overwhelming. This gathering is an effective way for the staff to have a chance to relax and browse the collection of new items.

 Janet Rowland, Brecksville-Broadview Heights High School,
Broadview Heights, Ohio
Library Media Connection • January 2004 (Volume 22, Issue 4)

OBTAINING
INPUT FROM TEACHERS

Help with Weeding & Collection Development

To get expert advice in collection development, I offered teachers in any department of the school their choice of books, worth $500, if they would help me "weed" books for at least two hours. That got me help with the weeding and selecting process.

Connie Weber, Churubusco (Indiana) Middle/High School
The Book Report • January/February 2000 (Volume 18, Issue 4)

Cooperative Weeding

Invite a different academic department into the library each month to go through the section(s) of the collection that apply to the curriculum. Encourage staff members to weed out and to suggest new titles for purchase. Offer food as an incentive. This works well on an every two- or three-year basis. It also gets people into the library who might not get there any other way.

Julie Burwinkel, Ursuline Academy, Cincinnati, Ohio
The Book Report • September/October 2000 (Volume 19, Issue 2)

Dream Grant

To convince teachers to take the time to suggest materials they would like for the library, print an official-looking personalized document stating that each has been awarded a $150 Dream Grant for the purchase of library materials for the school library. All they have to do is list the items they wish to have purchased or instead, just the subject matter. When the books arrive, make certain that each teacher receives "his" stack of books to look over before they are added to the library.

Sheryl Kindle Fullner, Nooksack Valley Middle School, Everson, Washington
Library Media Connection • October 2004 (Volume 23, Issue 2)

WORKING
TOGETHER

Library MOLE

No time for staff development? MOLE (mentoring online for excellence) can provide teachers with an effective tool for utilizing and investigating Web resources that enhance student learning. Initiate a brief e-mail to all teachers. In the e-mail, include one or two URLs for teachers to click on and investigate. Teachers, at a time convenient for them, are then exposed to a variety of sites and resources. Teachers can send a site suggestion back to the MOLE coordinator, who then features it in the MOLE system. Desktop staff development promotes educational objectives and is a great motivator for teachers, as technology becomes a tool for discovery.

Terry Zablocki, Boerne (Texas) High School
The Book Report • November/December 2001 (Volume 20, Issue 3)

Showcasing Student Work on the Web

Raise awareness of classroom and library partnerships. When showcasing student work on the Web, include information about the instructional unit for which the work was produced. Tell about research and other work done by the students. Elaborate on how students worked and how the product was created.

Debra Kay Logan, Mt. Gilead (Ohio) High School
Library Media Connection • February 2005 (Volume 23, Issue 5)

Circulation Cards

When you send materials to a teacher's classroom, make a circulation card for each book. Include call number, author, and title on book cards of a color you don't use for library materials. (I use yellow.) Send the cards with the materials to the teacher, who can use them to keep track of students borrowing these materials from the classroom. Keep the cards for future units. They are easier to update than a printed bibliography.

Cathy Keim, Meadowbrook (Pennsylvania) School
The Book Report • May/June 2001 (Volume 20, Issue 1)

Reservation Log

At our school we have a log in the media center where teachers sign up to use resources. The log has two parts. The first part is a calendar that lists each day and period with room to write in the class and number of students coming to the media center. The second part is a project sheet on which teachers identify what resources they need, items to reserve, and activities their students will be doing in the media center. This helps to limit the number of classes descending on the media center and lets us know when to restrict access to study hall. Teachers who need an idea for a unit or want to see what research projects and activities others are doing in the school can check the project sheets.

Rob Garter, Montville High School, Oakdale, Connecticut
Library Media Connection • August/September 2003 (Volume 22, Issue 1)

Teacher Files

Maintain a small file box with hanging files for each teacher who frequents the media center. In the file go the teacher's worksheets, your collaboration notes, Internet sites, etc. You can share teachers' ideas with others, and you can add other sources you uncover to the file.

Barbara Schiefler, Alvarado Middle School Media Center, Union City, California
Library Media Connection • November/December 2003 (Volume 22, Issue 3)

Writing Expectations

Consult a language arts teacher or a member of your district language arts curriculum committee to find out the writing grade level expectations. For example: Should they be using complex sentence structures? How many paragraphs with how many sentences should a sixth grader be expected to write? Share these skills while working with other subject areas teachers when students are creating written reports.

Debra Kay Logan, Mt. Gilead (Ohio) High School
Library Media Connection • March 2005 (Volume 23, Issue 6)

Examining Library Books

During exam week, offer teachers the opportunity to request a mobile book cart. Using a cart from the teacher's room or the library, check out a dozen or more books to the teacher. Before class begins, take the cart to the rooms. The teachers appreciate having the books available for those students who finish early.

Amy Nieters, Rappahannock County High School, Washington, Virginia
Library Media Connection • February 2005 (Volume 23, Issue 5)

Library Media Center Test Pass

If your school uses the library media center for make-up tests, know the "answers" to perennial test-taking questions in advance. Create a specific "Test Pass" for teachers to use when sending test-takers to the library media center. On the form, include a line for the student's name and places for the teacher to check if the student may not sit with others; use textbooks; use notes; use a calculator; or get help from the library media staff. A few lines for additional comments can also be helpful. Complete the pass design with spaces to note departure times and for adults to initial those times.

Taft Library Media Center Test Pass

Student's Name

Student is to sit alone _____.

Student may not:

_____ use textbook

_____ use notes

_____ use calculator

_____ request help from library/media staff

Additional comments:

_____

_____

Time left class: _____ Teacher's initials _____

Time left LMC _____ LMC staff initials _____

Deb Logan, Taft Middle School, Marion, Ohio

The Book Report • March/April 2000 (Volume 18, Issue 5)

INTEGRATING
CURRICULA

Desktop Patterns as Geography Lesson

Instead of the same old desktop patterns, we set the desktop patterns on our lab computers to pictures of different places in the United States and made a monthly contest out of guessing the locations. To start, we kept it simple and used easily identifiable places such as the Grand Canyon, Niagara Falls, the White House, etc. Students fill in the locations on a piece of paper, and correct entries are put into a drawing for prizes. This desktop lesson is something fun for the students that could be expanded to other topics (places in the world, animals, famous people, whatever). It could even tie in with a unit of study.

Jane Carlson, Ellis Middle School, Austin, Minnesota
The Book Report • September/October 2002 (Volume 21, Issue 2)

Acceptable Copying

Are your students researching foods from other countries or cultures? If so, this is the perfect time to discuss the few times it is acceptable to copy. Discuss why it is acceptable to copy a recipe. Ask questions such as, "Have you ever seen recipes that acknowledge their source?" An example would be a recipe such as Kay's Chocolate Marble Cookies.

Have them explain to you whether or not it would be legal to copy an entire recipe book. Why or why not?

Debra Kay Logan, Mt. Gilead (Ohio) High School
Library Media Connection • February 2005 (Volume 23, Issue 5)

Old Globes: New Mars

Most dusty school closets will yield an ancient out-of-date globe. (Old globes are also available at garage sales and thrift stores.) They are not old enough to be collectible, just old enough to be obsolete. We took our plastic globe and had students tear pieces of red, white, and orange tissue paper, which they glued on with decoupage medium. Then the students used the Internet and a NASA atlas to label the dried globe with major Martian features. Now that the two rovers have landed, we are adding those sites. Globes with broken supports can be suspended from the ceiling using clear fishing line.

 Sheryl Kindle Fullner, Nooksack Valley Middle School, Everson, Washington
Library Media Connection • March 2005 (Volume 23, Issue 6)

Adapted Lessons

When planning with cooperating teachers, don't forget to ask if any students will need to have lessons adapted.

 Debra Kay Logan, Mt. Gilead (Ohio) High School
Library Media Connection • April/May 2004 (Volume 22, Issue 7)

Lesson Plan Template

Teachers often need to write "formal lesson plans" for formal observations. Keep a lesson plan template on a computer so teachers can quickly type in the necessary information and print out a professional looking plan to provide to administrators or observers. You could also copy the template onto a disk for the teacher to use at home.

 Karen Eden, Old Mill High School, Millersville, Maryland
The Book Report • March/April 2000 (Volume 18, Issue 5)

Science Is a Shoe In

About once a year we hang clear plastic shoe bags from a tension rod in a library window. Students place items in the pockets that fit our current collection of shells, feathers, seeds/cones, leaves, nuts, or fossils (for safety's sake, no fungi!). Nature books are placed nearby to help students with identification. Students type or write the taxonomy and put it in the pocket with their specimens and their own names. In a leaf collection, younger students might specify "Box elder," while more advanced students would include the Latin "Acer negundo." After four weeks students vote for the most unusual specimen.

Sheryl Kindle Fullner, Nooksack Valley Middle School, Everson, Washington
Library Media Connection • February 2004 (Volume 22, Issue 5)

El Día de Los Muertos

To celebrate the Mexican Holiday "El Día de Los Muertos" (The Day of the Dead), collaborate with the advanced Spanish teacher at your high school to construct a bulletin board display in the media center. Students can design skeleton masks adorned with colored tissue, glitter, and sequins and create original tissue paper cuttings from kits purchased from a foreign language materials supplier. The creations make for a unique and appealing display that promotes cultural diversity.

Libby Bagby and Ann Bryant, North Surry High School, Mt. Airy, North Carolina
Library Media Connection • April/May 2004 (Volume 22, Issue 7)

Celebrate National Poetry Month

We set up a poetry wall in the library that wraps around a bank of circulation computers facing out into the LRC. Students use a colored erasable marker to write an original poem on this cartoon-fringed wall. Initials, first names, or full names are acceptable, but each poem has an identified author. In other locations around the LRC student lockers have "locker" poems that grace the locker doors. Students create an "Ode to My Locker" poem, which is written on a brightly colored sheet the size of their locker and decorated with original art or doodles for the artistically challenged. The culmination of National Poetry Month is a poetry slam entitled "A Night at the Blue Iguana Cafe," which features a café decorated LRC with tropical plants, spotlights, iridescent wall hangings, iguanas (not live!), a jazz quartet, and delicious cafe desserts and beverages. A student club provides both the food and the service while raising money for charitable organizations. The microphone is open to any age poet including parents, students, grandparents, and siblings. This series of events has grown over three years and attracts a large crowd of participants.

 Paulette Goodman, Kennedy Junior High School, Lisle, Illinois
Library Media Connection • March 2004 (Volume 22, Issue 6)

Vocabulary Treasure

To increase our students' vocabularies, we've introduced a "Vocabulary Word of the Day" during our televised morning announcements. Our students see the word, hear its meaning, and hear it used in two sentences. All of our teachers are encouraged to reinforce the word with their students throughout the day. Our media center posts the word on our circulation computer, as well. Then, the word is printed on a paper (with an official signature) and hidden somewhere in the building. The first person to find the paper, define the word, and use it correctly in a sentence wins a prize.

 Mary Gladwin, Hawthorne Junior High, Pocatello, Idaho
The Book Report • September/October 2002 (Volume 21, Issue 2)

Library-History Correlation

In our eighth grade, each student reads a dozen historical fiction books over the course of the school year. Correlating with each history unit at hand, these books help make history come alive and become memorable to the students. Classroom activities for each book ensure that students will read books in their entirety. Here are some suggested books:

Salem Witch Trials—*Beyond the Burning Time* by Lasky

Revolutionary War—*My Brother Sam Is Dead* by Collier

Voyageur books—*Broken Blade and Wintering* by Durbin

Lewis and Clark—*The Journal of Augustus Pelletier* by Lasky and *Seaman* by Karwoski

Factory Conditions in latter 1800s—*Ashes of Roses* by Auch

Civil War—*No Man's Land by Bartoletti* (South) and *Soldier's Heart* (North)

Racism—*Roll of Thunder, Hear My Cry* by Taylor

Transcontinental Railroad—*Dragon's Gate* (Central Pacific) by Yep and *The Journal of Sean Sullivan* (Union Pacific) by Durbin

 Connie Quirk, Mickelson Middle School, Brookings, South Dakota
Library Media Connection • February 2004 (Volume 22, Issue 5)

USING TECHNOLOGY IN THE LIBRARY

Computers, the ability to print, greater storage capacity, the ever-increasing World Wide Web, e-mail, on-line catalogs and cataloging, programs that allow for searching for and retrieval of information on the Internet, networking, and advances in programs for personal computers have led to a multitude of new applications—new ways that librarians can manage, teach, collaborate, promote reading, build positive public relations, and communicate with students, teachers, parents, and the public.

Technology-related tips in this section are divided into these topics:

- Computers
- Printing
- Web sites
- E-mail
- Cataloging
- Searching the Internet
- Useful Library Applications

COMPUTERS

Managing Floppy Disks

If students use library media center floppy disks to save work, a good way to manage the disks is by number. Starting with 1, write a large distinct number on each disk. When handing students disks for saving work, point out the disk's number and tell students that they will need to remember the number to find their work in the future. Having colored floppy disks makes remembering even easier. "I need disk orange 5!"

Deb Logan, Taft Middle School, Marion, Ohio
The Book Report • May/June 2001 (Volume 20, Issue 1)

It's in the Stars

In our library computer lab, we named each computer after a character in the zodiac. Each computer monitor bears a big label with its name (Sagittarius, Libra, Leo, etc.) and is identified on the network by that name. Students who want to use these computers check out a plastic pass, a paddle, matching a given computer. The paddle has a name label and barcode for easy checkout by our circulation system. Students love to ask for computers by name, and librarians can see at a glance that students are using the right computer.

Paul Scaer, J. R. Masterman Lab and Demonstration School,
    Philadelphia, Pennsylvania
The Book Report • January/February 2002 (Volume 20, Issue 4)

Tracking Computer Use in the Library

Need to keep track of computer use figures and also track which patrons used which computers? Excel is an excellent tool to track each day's transactions. Use a single spreadsheet for each month. Each column records a day's activity. When students come to the library to use the computers, have them pick up a slip with a computer station number on it, and scan their ID card with your barcode reader. The barcode number will be recorded in the spreadsheet cell. Because most barcodes have an embedded "enter" command, the cursor drops to the next cell in the column where you input the computer station number. At regular intervals include a time stamp (Control, Shift, Colon). It is easy at the end of the day to see how many computers were used. Simply divide the last row number by two. And you can search by computer number if you need to see the usage history for a specific computer.

David Bogardus, Diamond Ranch High School, Pomona, California
The Book Report • January/February 2002 (Volume 20, Issue 4)

The Multitasking Tip

When working on two programs simultaneously, my favorite speed tip is to use the "Alt" + "Tab" (Mac: "Command" + "Tab") combination to toggle between them. (Note: This is a favorite trick of students to hide a game they're playing by quickly switching to a program they're supposed to be working on.) It's easy to use this trick: Hold down the "Alt" key with your thumb, then press the "Tab" key with your index finger. Then, let go of the "Alt" key. This changes the program you're using to the last program that was accessed. To return to the first program, repeat the process. If you have multiple programs open, continue holding the "Alt" key down while pressing the "Tab" key. Notice that the selection device will toggle through icons representing all programs that are open. Release the "Tab" key at any time to open the selected icon.

Dusti Howell, Emporia (Kansas) State University
Library Media Connection • January 2003 (Volume 21, Issue 4)

Cleaning Computers

For cleaning computer keyboards of that "gooky gunk" (not dust) that accumulates from use by many fingers, try these:

- Alcohol on cotton swabs
- Glass cleaner on paper towel or sponge
- Pre-moistened wipes
- The dishwasher! (Definitely for Macintoshes, maybe for PCs)

Check manufacturer recommendations prior to trying any of these suggestions.

 Cindy Braun, Big Sky and Sentinel High School, Missoula, Montana
The Book Report • March/April 2001 (Volume 19, Issue 5)

Tangled Headphone Wires a Problem?

Headphone wires tangling and driving you crazy? Need a quicker fix than winding them up and putting a twist tie on them every time they're used?

Attach sticky back hooks to the side of each computer and hang the headphones on them. Variation: Tie up as much of the cord as possible with a twist tie leaving only enough cord to plug in the headphones and to reach the listener's ears. Leave one set by each computer.

Put the headsets in self-sealing plastic bags.

Use rubber bands, which secure cords easier and quicker than twist ties. Try these two items from the hardware store: A CableClamp® is an adjustable plastic clamp specifically designed to manage cables. The only problem is that five come in a package and only four of them are small enough. The other is quite a bit larger. The other item is a set of six "hobby spring clamps" made by Wolfcraft®. These are small plastic spring clamps just the right size to hold the wire together. Both of these items are quick and easy to use.

 Renee Choe-Winter, South East Junior High School, ICCSD, Iowa
Library Media Connection • March 2003 (Volume 21, Issue 6)

Facing Your Students

When you need to set up an LCD projector and computer on a cart when you want to maintain eye contact with the students, put the projector on the cart so it faces the screen and yourself. The computer and monitor also face the instructor so you are looking at the computer screen and the students at the same time. You can see the students while you use the mouse to move the cursor. If you have also used a smartboard, you have to turn your back to use it or to write on it, but this way you are always facing the class.

 Cheryl B. Adams, Patuxent High School, Lusby, Maryland
Library Media Connection • March 2003 (Volume 21, Issue 6)

Mice Lockdown

To protect optical mice and computer cables from being stolen, secure them by placing a plastic self-locking tie around the connecting cables and part of the hardware on the back of the CPU unit. Students may still pull cables out of the CPU but will not be able to remove them without being detected.

 Laura Jeanette Brown, Paint Branch High School, Hanover, Maryland
Library Media Connection • January 2006 (Volume 24, Issue 4)

"Your Students @ Your Library™" Display

Photos of students and events in your library are wonderful screen savers for the computers in your library. I've used photos of authors presenting in our library, students doing research, and kids working at our jigsaw puzzle table, but the most popular shots are of students having a wild time at after-school events in the library! Just take digital photos and save them to a floppy disk. Take the disk around to each computer and save a different photo as your screen saver on each monitor. Change the photos often!

 Laura Stiles, Cedar Valley Middle School, Round Rock ISD, Austin, Texas
Library Media Connection • April/May 2006 (Volume 24, Issue 7)

Wallpaper

Scan pictures of student artwork, the student of the month, individualized READ posters or pictures of student's individual interests and accomplishments and set them as the "wallpaper" on your library computers. Students love to see themselves and their friends displayed on the computer screens. This is a very popular feature of our library and excellent PR.

Suzanne Brown and Cara Russell, Parkview High School Library,
    Springfield, Missouri
Library Talk • January/February 2000 (Volume 13, Issue 1)

Copying Computer Screens into Documents

If you make brochures and presentations on how to use computer resources, teachers and students can benefit from a visual of the actual computer screen. To copy a computer screen into a document or PowerPoint presentation, go to the screen you want to copy and press **<control>** and **<print screen>** at the same time. Then go to your document or presentation and paste. You can then use the picture tool bar to crop the graphic to include only the part of the screen you need. Adding arrows to indicate the precise part of the screen you are describing really increases the effectiveness of the directions.

Karen Faulkenberry and Susan McNair, Lugoff-Elgin (South Carolina) High School
Library Media Connection • April/May 2005 (Volume 23, Issue 7)

Students As Teachers

Once you have shown a student how to do something on the computer, utilize his or her new expertise the next time another student needs help with the same problem or process. Teaching another student builds self-esteem and reinforces what the first student has learned.

Debra Kay Logan, Mt. Gilead (Ohio) High School
Library Media Connection • January 2005 (Volume 23, Issue 4)

What Is Today's Equivalent

To teach concepts reinforced by library usage, ask students to copy "new and improved" ads from *National Geographic* magazine from almost a century ago. They will find things like automobiles, central heat, traveling by ship to Europe, safety razors, coal furnaces—very mundane items—even union suits with only one button! Copy the pictures and have the children identify what the "new technology" in the ad was supposed to be. Some of them can't imagine that far back and will need help. Then ask them "What is today's equivalent?" Gives them a good idea that hot technology grows and changes.

Anne Shipley, Waterloo, New York
Library Media Connection • April/May 2004 (Volume 22, Issue 7)

PRINTING

Print Error Screen

Here's a way to swiftly communicate a problem to the local technology person or a software support agency at a distance. Press the <**control**> and the <**print screen**> keys simultaneously (<**print screen**> is usually above and to the right of the regular keyboard) while the error message is still on the screen. Then open a word processing document and press paste. Print out the copy, save for your records, and send the copy via e-mail to the technology person. The tech will be able to see exactly what error message you are receiving without your having to write it all down. The tech also will get other clues about what applications are currently open. When information on resolving the problem is received or discovered, type that into the word document along with the date. Place in a binder titled Tech Log. If the problem is encountered again, flipping through the error messages shows the solution.

 Sheryl Kindle Fullner, Nooksack Valley Middle School, Everson, Washington
Library Media Connection • February 2004 (Volume 22, Issue 5)

Printing Waste

A simple solution to students' wasteful printing habits is to quit stocking the printers with paper and provide students with a limited amount of sheets by request only. This keeps the T/L quite busy, but she is interacting with students; can suggest cut-and-paste, reducing, or clip art modifications; and can easily monitor which sites students are visiting to determine whether or not their print job is school-related.

 Sarah Werner, South Stokes High School, Walnut Cove, North Carolina
Library Media Connection • January 2003 (Volume 21, Issue 4)

Bibliographies for AR Collection

When students come in to select an AR book, they are sometimes overwhelmed by the huge selection, especially in the fiction area. From a jobber's Web site, make a list of AR books as if you were ordering them. (A competent student can do this work.) Then choose an annotated bibliography from their options and print out copies for each AR teacher. Put the bibliographies in a binder. The students enjoy browsing, and the teachers also have a better idea of what the books are about.

Anitra Gordon, Ypsilanti, Michigan
Library Media Connection • January 2005 (Volume 23, Issue 4)

Word Processing Point Size

Unless a teacher specifies otherwise, I tell students that all word processing done on library media center computers is with a size 14 point. The students are thrilled that they get to select a bigger point size than the default, and the size 14 helps out teachers with visual problems without being overly large.

Debra Kay Logan, Mt. Gilead (Ohio) High School
Library Media Connection • January 2005 (Volume 23, Issue 4)

Jobber Bibliographies

When you order books or videos using a company's Web site, find out if the site will print an annotated bibliography. If so, print bibliographies for the staff and to post on a New Book sign in the library.

Anitra Gordon, Lincoln High School, Ypsilanti, Michigan
Library Media Connection • November/December 2003 (Volume 22, Issue 3)

SITES

Web Page Title Placement

Be sure to place the title of a Web page at the top of the page to improve how some search tools list the page.

Debra Kay Logan, Mt. Gilead (Ohio) High School
Library Media Connection • April/May 2003 (Volume 21, Issue 7)

Increasing Web Page Accessibility

Increase the accessibility of your Web page by putting a period (punctuation mark) at the end of an image description in an ALT attribute. The period will give a person using a text reader a clearer reading and understanding of the contents of your Web site.

Debra Kay Logan, Mt. Gilead (Ohio) High School
Library Media Connection • October 2003 (Volume 22, Issue 2)

Web Site Maintenance

If you have a very large Web site to maintain, it can be extremely time-consuming to check for broken links on a regular basis. Use an automated link checker to check for dead or redirected links on your Web site. Xenu Link Sleuth is one example of such a program and is available for free at **<http://home.snafu.de/tilman/xenulink.html>**.

Amy Johnson, Swift Current Comprehensive High School,
Swift Current, SK, Canada
Library Media Connection • March 2004 (Volume 22, Issue 6)

Web Page Address Placement

When designing Web pages, remember it is helpful to put the address of the page itself in the footer with the signature and date. This makes citing the page simpler and provides an address if the page is found in the frame of another Web site.

 Debra Kay Logan, Mt. Gilead (Ohio) High School
Library Media Connection • January 2004 (Volume 22, Issue 4)

Finding a Web Site Address

Found a great site and want to create a link to it, but a frame of another site blocks the actual address of the great site? Use the "history" feature of the Web browser to uncover the actual address of a Web site accessed through a Web site frame.

 Debra Kay Logan, Mt. Gilead (Ohio) High School
Library Media Connection • November/December 2003 (Volume 22, Issue 3)

Annotating Web Links

Creating a Web page? When annotating your links, avoid including statistics about the site to which you are linking. If the link-to site has 550 links today, it may have 1,000 links next week. This is a maintenance nightmare.

 Debra Kay Logan, Mt. Gilead (Ohio) High School
Library Media Connection • April/May 2005 (Volume 23, Issue 7)

Storyboarding a Web Site

When storyboarding a Web site, use the storyboard to record page titles and page file names. Page names should reflect the content of the page.

 Debra Kay Logan, Mt. Gilead (Ohio) High School
Library Media Connection • January 2005 (Volume 23, Issue 4)

Clip Art Usage

When adding clip art to a Web page, keep careful records of the sources of all clip art. Record where the images are found and the corresponding usage restrictions and guidelines. Place copies of information about usage restrictions and copies of licenses in a file folder labeled "Image Use." Clearly label which clip art images are covered by the various licenses and guidelines.

 Debra Kay Logan, Mt. Gilead (Ohio) High School
Library Media Connection • February 2004 (Volume 22, Issue 5)

Linking to Web Sites

It is not necessary to ask permission to place a link on a Web site, but it may be beneficial to ask permission or to notify the Webmaster of the intention to link. Other Webmasters may add you to mailing lists in order to notify you in the event that their site undergoes substantial changes or moves to a new address. It is a good way to develop contacts with other educational Webmasters and can result in wonderful networking opportunities. When asking permission or notifying of intent to link, include the name and address of both your site and their site in the e-mail.

 Debra Kay Logan, Mt. Gilead (Ohio) High School
Library Media Connection • March 2004 (Volume 22, Issue 6)

E-MAIL

Clipping from E-mails

If you have Macs, a very useful, cheap, and small program developed by a Wisconsin college student is Net-Print, version 8.2 (Mac only). The program lets you "clip" super-fast from e-mail, Web pages, or whatever, and automatically picks up the URLs. I use Net-Print when I want to clip bits and pieces from e-mails of URLs and ideas I want to examine later, but I do not want to clutter my mailbox with a lot of saved e-mails. I have students use the program in the library when they need small portions of a Web page or several pages. Thus, they do not have to print the whole Web page. This saves time, paper, and ink when students need only bits and pieces from various sites. Net-Print is well worth the $10 cost, and is available from <**www.johnmoe.com/**>.

 Caroline Joiner, Sacred Heart HS, Hallettsville, Texas
The Book Report • September/October 2000 (Volume 19, Issue 2)

CATALOGING

Merging MARC Record Files

If you have several MARC record files (maybe with one record in each) and wish to get them into a single file to import into your automation system, follow these steps:

Click on Start and find Programs.

Then click on the MS-DOS prompt.

Be sure the disk you saved the records to is in drive A. Now type "A:" (don't type in the quotes) and press Enter.

Type "copy*.mrcfilename.mrc" (without the quotes). The filename is any word that you choose—just be logical. If your files have an extension of ".txt," you will type "copy *.txtfilename.txt" (without the quotes). Also, you need to write that filename somewhere so that you remember it. Press enter and the files will merge.

Click on the **X** in the upper right to Close and get back to where you were.

Now you can import the records into your cataloging program in the usual manner. When your program asks for the filename to import, you type in the filename you gave it when you merged the files.

 Dianne Davenport, B. F. Terry High School, Rosenberg, Texas
Library Media Connection • August/September 2003 (Volume 22, Issue 1)

Cataloging Easy Readers

Our high school library has some titles that we wanted to catalog as being an easier read than the rest of our collection. These volumes aren't specifically high-interest/low-vocabulary books, although a few of them may be. They may simply be shorter or at a lower reading level. We decided to catalog these books as "Quick Reads" in the MARC cataloging (650 subject heading) so that they're searchable in the computerized catalog. We're also using green spine labels for these materials so that they're easily spotted on the shelving amidst the white labels. This labeling is clear, and the kids who need it are clued in to the concept, but it isn't so blatant as to make reluctant readers even more reluctant to take out or use an "easy" book. Another advantage is that even students who are avid readers sometimes look for a quick read.

 Amy Johnston, Swift Current Comprehensive High, Saskatchewan, Canada
Library Media Connection • April/May 2003 (Volume 21, Issue 7)

Record Summaries

I often write catalog record summaries for books whose MARC records arrive without them. But sometimes the summaries we do get can invite frustration and wasted time: "As summer ended and 17-year-old Patrick looked forward excitedly to his senior year at Dickinson High, his father announced he'd been transferred, and the family would be moving from their small New England town to the large city of Buffalo, New York..." In my library, this innocent YA novel will pop up among the hits for keyword searches that kids may be doing on St. Patrick, Patrick Henry, the poems of Emily Dickinson, jolly old England, or the fate of the American buffalo. If time allows, I do a quick rewrite without all those unnecessary proper names: "As summer ended and a 17-year-old boy looked forward excitedly to his senior year in high school, his father announced he'd been transferred, and the family would be moving from their small town to a large city in another state..."

 Dana Lehrman, Jane Addams Vocational High School, Bronx, New York
The Book Report • March/April 2001 (Volume 19, Issue 5)

Improving Library Cataloging

The most useful materials in the world will remain on the shelf, unused, if the library's catalog database is not user-friendly. A database is only as good as its material tracings and summaries, but because companies are cutting cataloging costs, at least two-thirds of the materials I order arrive without summaries, tracings, or both. I create my own summaries and tracings for the library's catalog using chapter titles and indexes for nonfiction books and book-related sites on the Internet for fiction and sometimes nonfiction books. I also keep book reviews as I prepare my order, file these reviews alphabetically by author after the books arrive, and refer to them when writing summaries.

Jeanette Roberts, Moundridge (Kansas) High School
The Book Report • September/October 2000 (Volume 19, Issue 2)

Swift Shelving

Even with an online cataloging provider, many free or reissued books that we receive are slow to make their way into the catalog. To provide a stopgap measure, we bookmarked our countywide library system catalog. We look for an identical or close match to the book in hand, pirate the Dewey number, and then add the first three letters of the author's last name instead of a Cutter number. This method lets us get the books onto the shelves swiftly. Because these entries are typed all in caps, it's easy to upgrade them to full cataloging in batches as information becomes available for download.

Sheryl Kindle Fullner, Nooksack Valley Middle School, Everson, Washington
The Book Report • September/October 2002 (Volume 21, Issue 2)

History Magazines as References

I catalog and enter each issue of four different history magazines (*Calliope, Faces, Cobblestone,* and *Footsteps*) into our automated circulation system. We shelve them in the magazine room just like other periodicals. They are wonderful publications and come in handy when we need additional resources. Students can access them by title or subject. Schools may choose to circulate the periodicals or keep them as reference tools. We do not circulate them, and we have issues dating back to 1990.

Laura J. Viau, Monroe Middle School, Rochester, New York
The Book Report • November/December 2001 (Volume 20, Issue 3)

Temporary Catalog Records

Sometimes MARC records are not available for ancient books, used books, too new books. When I want to get books on the shelf in a hurry, I do a quick, very abbreviated catalog record with just title, author, call number, and publishing info. I don't want to leave the record like that permanently, so I do these fast entries ALL IN CAPS, which not only allows me to type faster but also leaves a visual trail that I can pick up quickly when I scroll through that section of our collection. It also alerts me to the absence of added entries, etc., if that's what I'm looking for. I also type NFC in a field I don't use so that I can do a global search for a batch of these Not Fully Catalogued items to update them when time permits. I type DLF for Don't Look Further on items that will probably never have records, such as some vanity-published books or old classics for which finding the correct edition out of hundreds would require hours of searching.

Sheryl Kindle Fullner, Nooksack Valley Middle School, Everson, Washington
The Book Report • January/February 2002 (Volume 20, Issue 4)

SEARCHING
THE INTERNET

Speedier Internet Searches

To reduce the time it takes each new screen to load when you're on the Internet, turn off image loading. With Netscape Navigator, you do this under the options menu, by clicking to take the check off of auto load image. If you are using a regular phone line, a slower modem, or if you don't need to see the graphics, this will speed the rate at which each new screen loads. You can always click on any graphic you want to see to bring it up.

Sharon Sellars, East Paulding Middle School, Dallas, Georgia
The Book Report • March/April 2000 (Volume 18, Issue 5)

Web Site Resource List

Our faculty has begun to use the Internet more and more in the last two years. I created a Web site resource list for several units, including The Great Depression, Fad Diets, and Diseases. I keep a copy of those lists in a three ring binder. I have begun to print out HIT lists from LM_NET of Web site resources. I give a copy to the appropriate teacher and keep a copy to put in the Web site resource binder. I also include information on citing electronic resources from Classroom Connect and MLA.

Kay Goss, Mansfield R-IV Schools, Mansfield, Missouri
The Book Report • January/February 2001 (Volume 19, Issue 4)

Copernic

If you have PCs, the Copernic program searches multisearch engines at once and allows you to check the result entries you want to explore. It then places them in a browser page as hot links, which you can save as an icon on the desktop. This speeds up the student's searching, allows you or the teacher to filter the search results, and is easier to handle than bookmarks. Copernic is available from **www.download.com**. This is a PC program only.

Caroline Joiner, Sacred Heart High School, Hallettsville, Texas
The Book Report • January/February 2001 (Volume 19, Issue 4)

URL Address Book

To help us navigate the oceans of information on the Internet, I started a URL address book—in a REAL address book kept on my desk. I included only addresses of "tried and true" best Web sites. The address book will fold back, and many times I just hand the book to the student for them to type in the URL if they are lost in the storm of research. This enables me to work with many students at once. Several of our teachers have said what a great idea they thought the address book was. It certainly helps from year to year to be able to find that 'perfect' research site again.

Anna Lee, Swanson Middle School, Arlington, Virginia
Library Media Connection • January 2003 (Volume 21, Issue 4)

Past Project Links

After pulling together an online project page of links, do not discard the links when the project is over. Create a file of past project page entries. Better yet, have an Internet Archive Page of past projects.

Debra Kay Logan, Mt. Gilead (Ohio) High School
Library Media Connection • October 2003 (Volume 22, Issue 2)

Send 'em to the Web

For frequent research topics, instead of giving handouts of URLs for biomes, or countries, or holidays, etc., create a Web page with all the topic URLs. The Web index page is the main table of contents. The student chooses his topic from the table of contents and hyperlinks to the sites of his choice. You can easily keep adding topics to the contents page, and the students don't have to worry about correctly typing and spelling the URL.

Deborah Dick, Kickapoo High School, Springfield, Missouri
Library Media Connection • August/September 2004 (Volume 23, Issue 1)

Print AND Online

When you work with a class on a research project, you often suggest helpful Web sites for them to use. Rather than have students write the URLs by hand (and possibly record them incorrectly), give them a custom made bookmark. Students appreciate having something to mark their spot in a book and a quick reference for Internet use during study hall or at home.

Jenni Seibel, D.C. Everest Middle School, Weston, Wisconsin
Library Media Connection • October 2004 (Volume 23, Issue 2)

U S E F U L
LIBRARY APPLICATIONS

Promoting the Print Collection

We're using technology to promote our print collection. When students read any of our new books, I ask them if they'd like to write a very short review for the bottom of the library Web page. We scan in pictures of the book jackets (with permission, of course) and use four or five at a time. When anyone clicks on a picture, an enlarged image comes up, along with the review signed with the student's name (first name only). I have built up a file of reviews, so we can change the page every few weeks.

 Nancy Van Dinter, Bishop Kelly High School, Boise, Idaho
The Book Report • January/February 2000 (Volume 18, Issue 4)

Online Selection Tools

Looking for books on a particular subject? Are your standard CD-ROM selection tools limited in what they index? I've found amazon.com to be a great resource for finding books on particular subjects. Amazon.com tends to have a better selection of high school- and adult-level books than my CD-ROM databases, plus they provide book reviews and customer comments for many of the books. I've also found their links to related titles of interest to be very helpful. Other online booksellers, such as barnesandnoble.com and borders.com, are also helpful, but I've found amazon.com to be the easiest and fastest to use, and I like the setup and features of their database the best.

 Amy M. Pritzl, Southern Door County High School, Brussels, Wisconsin
The Book Report • May/June 2000 (Volume 19, Issue 1)

Accelerated Reader

Our English department encourages reading by using the "Accelerated Reader" program. To help the students quickly access the books that are available, I have added "Accelerated Reader" as the subject in our automated system. By typing "Accelerated Reader," an entire list is provided, and students can tell at a glance which ones are available.

Connie Spurlock, Wm. H. Harrison (Ohio) High School
The Book Report • May/June 2000 (Volume 19, Issue 1)

Easy Scheduling

You keep a deskpad calendar for class scheduling, but you don't memorize it. Why not make scheduling easier by keeping your media center schedule online? If your school Web page doesn't have room, try **myschoolonline.com**, a free Web site where you can set up such a calendar along with other information. You'll be able to go to any available computer and schedule on the spot.

Robert L. Otte, South Christian High School, Grand Rapids, Michigan
The Book Report • January/February 2002 (Volume 20, Issue 4)

Photo Circulation

Our catalog software allows us to include photographs of the items in the records, so we plan to include digital photos of some of our kits. Once upgraded to the latest version of our software, we will use the 856 tag to include photos of items within the catalog record.

Kathy Graves, Siskiyou County Office of Education, Yreka, California
The Book Report • March/April 2002 (Volume 20, Issue 5)

Notable Student Teachers

When I evaluate student teachers I use my computer to take notes of their performance. I often ask them questions in the notes. Since it is sometimes hard to find time to conference with the student teacher, at their convenience they read the notes and answer the questions using italics. I then have a file copy of my observation of the student teacher.

Gregg Miles, Ebenezer Middle School, Effingham County, Georgia
Library Media Connection • March 2003 (Volume 21, Issue 6)

PowerPoint Picture Albums

Using Microsoft PowerPoint XP, you can make a slide-show presentation by inserting a lot of pictures at once, rather than inserting one picture at a time. I make a weekly PowerPoint slide show of kids and things happening at our school. With previous versions of PowerPoint you had to go to File — Insert Picture — Find the File (where the pictures are), then click on the single picture, insert it, and drop-and-drag it to fit the slide. In XP, however, you can go to File — Insert Picture, then insert Photo Album, which allows you to "Find" the folder where you save your pictures, then insert the entire file of pictures. After "Insert," choose "Create," and voila — you have a slide show. Employing this technique can save hours of time.

Kathi Worthy, Paulding County High School, Dallas, Georgia
Library Media Connection • April/May 2003 (Volume 21, Issue 7)

AR Lists on the Web

Exporting the books and quizzes from the program to a file is very easy if you have AR Book Guide. The directions can be found in the manual, using "help" in the management program, or calling customer service. What happens after you export the list depends on the software you have for your site.

Karen Brostad, Bennington (Nebraska) Public Schools
Library Media Connection • March 2003 (Volume 21, Issue 6)

Shared Information

To share questions, concerns, and articles without having to copy, compile, and re-compile masses of information, create a shared folder on your network. Each person affected, regardless of what building they are in, may access this electronic folder of information and add to it. To prevent accidental deletion, allow only one person access to delete information. This folder may contain a Word document that addresses questions and concerns of all. Each person may add to this document. Another document can summarize meetings, evaluations, etc. When you find articles in professional magazines on the Internet, add them to this folder also for each member to read. Everything is available at the click of the mouse, thus saving much time searching for information you know you already have.

Donna Walters, Valparaiso (Indiana) High School
Library Media Connection • April/May 2005 (Volume 23, Issue 7)

Clip Art Collection

If you collect clip art, put it in folders labeled with the sources you use. In each folder, copy each source's stipulations for using their clip art and the URL for the site into a word processing document. In this way, you can use the clip art in the future and won't have to wonder where it came from or if there were guidelines for using it. You might also create a database so that you can easily search for certain types of clip art in your source folders.

Cathy Hart, Perry Middle School, Worthington, Ohio
The Book Report • March/April 2001 (Volume 19, Issue 5)

Remote Access Services

If you travel to conferences or vacation and you need to access your office computer from the road, try one of the remote access services. "GoToMyPC" is an example. For about $20 for a month of access, you can open your library database as well as any database subscriptions. Anything you can access from your office computer including PowerPoint and word processing files, can also be accessed from the beach, a convention, a hotel, a seminar, or Internet cafe.

 Sheryl Kindle Fullner, Nooksack Valley Middle School, Everson, Washington
Library Media Connection • April/May 2004 (Volume 22, Issue 7)

Pathfinder Replacement

If you create a Pathfinder of links to appropriate sites for a class project and place it on your Web page, that page may not always be available. Create the pathfinder as an MS Word document on the network server. Students can access the Pathfinder, click on the links, and get to the sites they need much more quickly than if they had to type in the URLs.

 Holly Tesar, Excelsior Springs (Missouri) High School
Library Media Connection • October 2004 (Volume 23, Issue 2)

PROMOTING
READING

Every day in every way, librarians promote reading. In displays, in direct contact with students, in teaching research skills, through technology, in public relations, when purchasing books, the motivating intent is to bring students in contact with books and information. Reading is "what we're about."

Tips in this section address:

- Booktalks
- Displays and Bulletin Boards
- Reading Incentives
- Student Recommendations
- Special Events
- Special Tactics
- Utilizing Technology

BOOKTALKS

Booktalks with Visual Aids

Sixth graders love booktalks. To cover as many books as possible in one class period, set up four rectangular tables end-to-end in the front of the library media center. Create a backdrop for the books using a variety of shapes and sizes of empty boxes draped with colorful plastic sheeting. Place your new fiction books to be shared on bookstands at various elevations on the tables. Accompany each with an item representing the storyline. For example, Lasky's Ga'Hoole series can have a stuffed toy owl and an owl call; *The Tale of Despereaux* can have a stuffed mouse with exaggerated felt ears. As you deliver your talk, have a helper parade in front of the watchful students with each book and item. The next day, get your reading teachers to ask the students, as a class, to recall as many of the items as possible in five minutes. Give prizes to the class with the best score. Multiple copies of your new titles will cover demand.

Connie Quirk, G. S. Mickelson Middle School, Brookings, South Dakota
Library Media Connection • February 2006 (Volume 24, Issue 5)

Recorded Booktalks

Many companies that sell recorded books have sample readings available at the click of a mouse. I turn my computer volume control up to fill the library media center space and then pick a popular new book. The sample chapter rolls out in sonorous or stentorian tones of the professional reader. Students are mesmerized. Some have even missed part of their lunchtime to listen to the readings. This serves as a free booktalk even while I am busy with circulation.

Sheryl Fullner, Nooksack Valley Middle School, Everson, Washington
Library Media Connection • August/September 2005 (Volume 24, Issue 1)

Scary Booktalks

When asked to booktalk to students, divide mystery/suspense/scary books into two categories as you present: realistic and supernatural. Before you begin the actual talks, lead the class in a discussion of which elements they might expect to find in each category, and continue to discuss which category they think is scarier. This can get rather lively as students have strong divided opinions! (Some of your families may not want their children reading books with supernatural elements, and this method helps those students make informed choices.) As you show the books, also ask the students why they think there are more girls/women than boys/men on the covers. The response is "because girls get scared easier," to which the girls will vocally protest. Then talk about publishers putting images on the cover that they think will help sell the book. After this, the guys don't seem so shy about picking up a book with a girl on the cover.

When you present booktalks on science fiction and fantasy books, before you begin, go over definitions of the two genre. List elements that they might find in each genre. Discuss books they've read and movies they've recently seen, as this actually adds to the definition of science fiction and fantasy. As you talk about each book or certain authors, categorize fantasy or science fiction. Students have told me they appreciate this way of presentation because it helps them find books they will want to read.

Carol A. Burbridge, Jardine Middle School, Topeka, Kansas
Library Media Connection • October 2005 (Volume 24, Issue 2)

Book Talk Requests

When doing book talks to students, give each student a 3x5 card (I use old catalog cards) and have them put their name and student number on the card. As you talk about books, have them write on the card the title of the book they want to put on reserve. At the end of class, collect the cards. Back to the library, you have the information you need to put books on reserve for them. This process will save students having to come to the library later to request the book.

Mary Ann Reese, Xenia (Ohio) Central Middle School
Library Media Connection • April/May 2006 (Volume 24, Issue 7)

Rotating Booktalks

Even after purchasing a fair-sized collection of novels, most media centers are unlikely to have enough copies of a book to booktalk the same titles for several classes in one day. If six English classes are scheduled to hear booktalks and check out books, for instance, you need booktalks for six sets of books. These same students will be back in a few weeks to hear about more books, which can create confusion about which books you've shared with each class. Try presenting a different literary genre during each period, then rotating the schedule every six weeks so that all classes hear all the genre presentations.

Betty Stone, Providence Day School, Charlotte, North Carolina
The Book Report • January/February 2000 (Volume 18, Issue 4)

Readers' Send-Off

Send your graduating middle school students to high school with a mission to read! Near the end of the school year, carefully select books from your area's high school library media centers. Choose an intriguing collection of fiction and nonfiction. Include some old favorites that can be found in both your and the high school libraries. Entice the soon-to-be high school students by including books that are "too old" for your library's collection. Schedule times to booktalk the books. Send them off anxious to visit their "new" library media center.

Deb Logan, Taft Middle School, Marion, Ohio
The Book Report • May/June 2001 (Volume 20, Issue 1)

DISPLAYS
AND BULLETIN BOARDS

Book Jacket Mural

Students can create murals to advertise "good reads" available in the LMC. Using book jackets, students choose those jackets that appeal to them and read the blurbs summarizing the stories on the inside of the covers. In small groups, they design an overall advertisement for the books they choose, using a billboard-like design to attract attention. Collaborate with the art teacher on this project to "spice up" monthly book displays and to encourage students to discover new titles in the library.

Connie Cleary, Edison Middle School, Green Bay, Wisconsin
Library Media Connection • November/December 2004 (Volume 23, Issue 3)

Reading Wall

Set up an ongoing "Reading Wall" that displays jackets of students' favorite books. Each grading period, focus on titles favored by students in a different grade. For example, we featured the senior class the first nine weeks of school, the junior class the second nine weeks, etc., but the idea works for any grade. Students write a two-to-three-sentence review of their favorite books (without giving away the ending) and three words/phrases/questions that literally describe the book. In addition to the book jacket and review, post the name of the student who recommends the book. The wall is ongoing in that students can contribute to it even if their grade has already been featured.

Nancy Keenan, Glenvar High School, Salem, Virginia
Library Media Connection • April/May 2003 (Volume 21, Issue 7)

Books of the Week Display

This year, we had a window display called "Books of the Week." Our teachers and staff chose books and items to complement the material. What fun it is to find a sports person who shows championship Pekinese or another teacher who has a collection of *Wizard of Oz* memorabilia.

Carol Strope, Fairmont Junior High School, Boise, Idaho
The Book Report • January/February 2000 (Volume 18, Issue 4)

Reading Motivation Display

In our media center we have a book security system that seemed out of place with our inviting reading atmosphere. We purchased a six-foot, tri-fold photo screen and inserted book cover jackets instead of photos in the picture windows. The result was a reading motivation display that hid our security system at the same time. We plan to change book covers as we purchase new books.

Louise Scott and Kathey Davidson, Creekland Middle School,
   Lawrenceville, Georgia
The Book Report • September/October 2000 (Volume 19, Issue 2)

READ Mini-Posters

We stirred a lot of student and faculty interest with our READ mini-posters (an ALA poster take-off) featuring our own students, teachers, staff, and custodians photographed with their favorite books. We displayed the faculty and staff posters in the library and students' pictures on three bulletin boards in the hallways. When we started photographing student library workers for the series, we had others volunteering to have their pictures on the bulletin boards. All we needed was a digital camera, computer and software, regular copy machine paper, and a laminating machine.

Petty Gandolfo and Dee Parks, Madison Central High School, Richmond, Kentucky
The Book Report • May/June 2001 (Volume 20, Issue 1)

Caught Reading

Prepare a bulletin board entitled "We Are Reading, Too!" to introduce students to faculty and staff. Photograph each staff member and mount the picture along with the name, grade level, or team and a short comment about a book the staff member has recently enjoyed. Students and faculty enjoy looking at the pictures and reading about recommended books. After a couple of weeks, ask students to add their book recommendations and "Join Us."

 Norma Jones, Bessemer City (North Carolina) Middle School
Library Media Connection • February 2003 (Volume 21, Issue 5)

High School Quick Reads

I keep several magazine shelves next to our magazine section for our students' favorite quick reads. *Guinness Book of World Records, I Spy*™, sports' photo books, *The Far Side*® comic books, and other special features that come and go, such as *The Osbournes, Mad Magazine Special Edition, Sports Bloopers*, and various photography books, keep the section busy. The section is great for those students sent to the library media center awaiting discipline or meetings. These books are, without a doubt, the most read books in the library media center!

 Kim Clynch, Harleton (Texas) ISD Library
Library Media Connection • January 2006 (Volume 24, Issue 4)

Promoting Reading

To promote literacy throughout your school, establish a permanent "Reading" bulletin board. Ask teachers for a personal photograph taken when they were in middle school, along with the title of a book they enjoyed reading as a teen. Display these "Once upon a time . . . we read, too" selections during your school's fall open house. Parents and students will enjoy seeing teachers as teen readers!

Barbara Hirsch, Hastings Middle School, Upper Arlington, Ohio
Library Media Connection • January 2006 (Volume 24, Issue 4)

Book of the Month

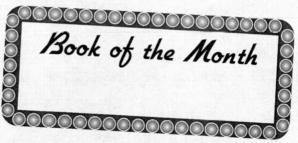

In order to help students and teachers to become aware of the books in our library collection, I made a display called Book of the Month. I purchased a wooden painter's easel for about $15 and foam cork board. With Print Shop, I made a big sign that reads: "Book of the Month." A book with a short blurb is placed on the easel. A copy of the book cover is also placed on the easel if a student checks the book out. Students can check out the book for one week.

Sue Dwars, Andrean High School, Merrillville, Indiana
Library Talk • January/February 2000 (Volume 13, Issue 1)

R E A D I N G
INCENTIVES

Rewarding Accelerated Readers

Our school uses Accelerated Reader, and quizzes are administered in the library. We generate a "Top Point-Earners Report" on the last day of each marking period. We give the report to teachers to post, and the top three AR point-earners in the ninth grade and the top three in the 10th grade are awarded "Good Readership," $15 gift certificates donated by local bookstores.

Pat Berry, Chatham High School, Chatham, New Jersey
The Book Report • May/June 2002 (Volume 21, Issue 1)

Free Reading Incentives

Some FREE incentives for students that you can use with reading incentive programs include:

- First in lunch line pass
- Free homework, tardy, and/or hall pass
- Sit in teacher's chair for one class period
- Create bulletin board for a teacher
- Lunch with a teacher
- Teacher aid for one class period

These incentives proved to be a hit with both the middle school students and the school's pocket book!

Angela Vietti O'Kane, Montieello Trails Middle Schoo,l Shawnee, Kansas
Library Media Connection • March 2003 (Volume 21, Issue 6)

Choosing AR Books

If your school uses an automated reading assessment program like Accelerated Reader, talk with students about selecting a book by the reading level at which they are comfortable instead of by the book's number of points. Ask them how many points they are likely to get if they do not understand what they are reading.

Debra Kay Logan, Mt. Gilead (Ohio) High School
Library Media Connection • April/May 2005 (Volume 23, Issue 7)

Atomic Champion Reading Success

At our middle school, students can earn reading incentives that are funded by PTA and local businesses. After a basic reading requirement of three books per grading period, students reading an additional book earn Bronze-level status (a fast food coupon), with Silver (school ice cream coupon), Gold (free mini-golf game), Platinum (drawing for mall gift certificate), and Titanium (free aquatic center ticket) for greater numbers. The highest level, Atomic Champion, is for those students who read at least nine books per grading period and pass comprehension quizzes for them. Atomic Champions are invited to the media center for a pizza café lunch served by the school's administrators.

Louise Scott and Betsy Simmons, Creekland Middle School,
    Lawrenceville, Georgia
Library Media Connection • August/September 2004 (Volume 23, Issue 1)

STUDENT
RECOMMENDATIONS

Book Feedback Forms

When a class comes in to select books for outside readings, give the teacher a stack of "Book Feedback Forms," half-sheets with space for the author, title, and a few lines for comments about the book. Ask the teachers if they would have their students fill them out when they finish their books. You will get great feedback on the books they read, and sometimes good ideas for new books for the library. Best of all, you get some great student quotations to read along with booktalks for future classes!

Tish Carpinelli, Lower Cape May Regional High School, Cape May, New Jersey
Library Media Connection • August/September 2004 (Volume 23, Issue 1)

Recommended Reading

High school students are always grazing the shelves of our YA fiction collection for a good read. To make it quick and easy to find a great book, put the title, author, genre, and plot summary of each of your most popular books on a 3" x 5" index card in a small inexpensive photo album. This way the students can flip through to find a book that interests them. You can also encourage students to write their comments about the book on the bottom of the card to help other readers.

Alisha Wisniewski, North Kansas City (Missouri) Public Library/High School
Media Center
Library Media Connection • February 2005 (Volume 23, Issue 5)

Reading Favorites

Close to the end of the school year, ask your current middle school sixth graders to fill out a half page form. On it, ask students to share in two or three complete sentences their favorite book read in the past school year and why. Categorize the hits into categories: Fantasy, Mystery and Suspense, Real Life Situations, and Sports, typing the titles under the appropriate category. Select a few comments and type these on the back of the reading list but without the students' names. That way it will be the books that are highlighted and not particular students. You can hand out these lists to current sixth graders for summer reading recommendations, and you can give the list to incoming sixth graders next fall as books recommended by their peers.

Connie Quirk, Mickelson Middle School, Brookings, South Dakota
Library Media Connection • February 2005 (Volume 23, Issue 5)

Personalized Book Selection

When small resource classes with a variety of reading levels come to the library media center for book selection, ask the teacher to have the students fill out index cards with their name and three subjects they might be interested in reading about. Have the teacher jot down an approximate reading level on each card before he or she gives them to you. Use the cards to select books for individual students, and when the classes come to the library media center, have the books ready to offer the students. Keep the cards throughout the school year so you have their interests in mind when ordering.

Tish Carpinelli, Lower Cape May Regional High School, Cape May, New Jersey
Library Media Connection • October 2005 (Volume 24, Issue 2)

Student Approved

I maintain a notebook of simple student reviews in the library media center. For each of the favorable reviews, I fold an index card in half lengthwise and write on the outside: Recommended by student's name. I note the title and call # on the inside of the card for future use. I prop the card on the outside cover of the book on display. It is amazing to see those recommended books fly off the shelves. As an added bonus, students are eager to write more reviews so they can see their recommended book on display. I was able to create a check-in note in our circulation program to alert me when one of the recommended books was returned, so I can easily display it again with its card.

 Marcia Krantz, Hudson Falls (New York) Middle School
Library Media Connection • January 2006 (Volume 24, Issue 4)

SPECIAL
EVENTS

Summer Reading Sources

Each year, my district's English, social studies, and science teachers assign a list of books for summer reading for students coming into grades 9 through 12. Last year, my high school library media center held a special Summer Reading List "book fair" just before school let out in June. Each class visited us for half a period, during which we displayed the library's copies of the reading list books and briefly booktalked them, so students would know a little about the books from which they could choose. (Length, of course, was of prime interest.) Since I "moonlight" at the local public library as well, I stressed the importance of beating the end-of-summer rush on the most popular titles. I especially recommended that students who would be going away for the summer, or who tended to run up overdue fines, might want to consider their own copies of the books. We had negotiated with a local bookseller to obtain reasonable prices, which were passed on to the students. They placed orders with us during the week of the book fair and paid up front. The bookseller delivered the requested titles well before the end of the school year, and the library staff connected students with their books during final exam week. In September, several students expressed their thanks for this convenient service, which they hoped would be continued in future years.

 Catherine M. Andronik, Brien McMahon High School, Norwalk, Connecticut
Library Media Connection • March 2003 (Volume 21, Issue 6)

Reading Banquet

Host a Reading Banquet. Each reading class uses the theme of a different book to decorate an eight-foot table with placemats, mint cups, bookmarks, and centerpieces. Arrange the tables, which can include everything from *The Cat in the Hat* to *Charlotte's Web* to *Holes*, in the school gymnasium or other large room. Charge students, families, and community members about $5 to view the tables and attend the banquet. Students can serve generous desserts, prepared by teachers. Other students can provide musical performances, read poetry, or write and perform book skits. It will be a great family night for your school and can raise funds for your library media center. We make ours an annual event!

Bev Gustafson, Lexington (Nebraska) Middle School
Library Media Connection • August/September 2005 (Volume 24, Issue 1)

Readers' Forum

To get student input on book selection and purchases, start a "Readers' Forum." Begin with about 20 students who you know are avid readers. Invite them to lunch in the library and ask them to be prepared to talk briefly about two books that they have enjoyed (or not enjoyed as the case may be). Other than just devouring pizza, many students find their reading "soul mates" through these forums. They also get ideas for independent reading projects and recreational reading, find a great place to spout off about their favorite books, and help you really get to know your readers and know that they like the books you've purchased. After the various sessions of forums, compile a brochure listing all of the titles and whether your library owns them. One page of the brochure can contain a survey that asks them to recommend another reader friend to add to your forums. You can also have one of your Web-savvy aides create a Web page with brief summaries of each book.

Victoria E. Blaser, Tiverton (Rhode Island) High School
Library Media Connection • November/December 2005 (Volume 24, Issue 3)

SPECIAL
TACTICS

Reading Fantasy Series in Order

Fantasy books are frequently written in a series. Because we witnessed a dramatic increase in fantasy reading, I devised a system to help the students read the books in order. I wrote the number of the series on the top of the book. For example, on *The Great Hunt* by Robert Jordan, I wrote the number "2." Now students see at a glance which book comes next.

Eileen B. Jones, Hillcrest High School, Simpsonville, South Carolina
The Book Report • September/October 2001 (Volume 20, Issue 2)

Fantasy Series

Do you struggle to remember the order of the many fantasy series out there? Type up a two-sided handout that contains favorite fantasy authors, with titles listed in series order. Put copies on a rotating stand on the checkout counter. Students like to check off books read and now have many suggestions at their fingertips.

Connie Quirk, G. S. Mickelson Middle School, Brookings, South Dakota
Library Media Connection • February 2006 (Volume 24, Issue 5)

Read Alouds

When classes come to the media center for book checkout, always read them the first chapter of a book. If they are looking for a particular genre (historical fiction, fantasy, mystery, etc.) then the read-aloud would be one of those. If they are in for a general checkout, find a title you have multiple copies of, but that hasn't moved much recently. Or read them one of the year's state reading program nominees. One chapter is enough to get the students hooked and yet allows enough time afterward for browsing and checkout.

 Barbara Schiefler, Alvarado Middle School Media Center, Union City, California
Library Media Connection • November/December 2003 (Volume 22, Issue 3)

Summer Book Out

Send your library media center books on summer vacation. Students really appreciate access to your collection over the summer when they have more time to read. The Advanced Placement English students, for example, choose titles from the recommended list to prepare for the fall. Many take home the books they just couldn't find time to read during the school year. Simply set up a special due date two to three weeks into the next school year and check out the books. Advertise with a summer theme such as "Books for the Beach" or "Reading Fun in the Sun." Ask each student to sign a simple agreement and write down the number of books he or she takes home. Place a return box in the school office so that students can return the books over the summer. We started slowly by setting a limit of ten books, but now allow a maximum of 20 books per student. We have checked out more than 1,200 books over the past 12 years for summer reading, with very few problems.

 Patricia Eloranta, Medford (Wisconsin) Area Senior High School
Library Media Connection • January 2006 (Volume 24, Issue 4)

Middle School Lit Requests

Middle school students often request books of a specific type, such as tear-jerkers, humorous books, sports fiction, teen pregnancy fiction, child abuse fiction, fast page turners, etc. It is not always easy to think of a recommendation on the spur of the moment. Keep a three-ring binder with lists related to issues teens ask about. Each time you finish reading a book, add the title and author to one of the lists.

Mavis Schipman, Douglas Middle School Library, Box Elder, South Dakota
Library Media Connection • March 2006 (Volume 24, Issue 6)

Book Review File

Keep an index card file box and a supply of index cards available for students to complete mini book reviews. Information on the cards can include title, author, call number, a sentence or two about the book, a rating system (such as a letter grade or number of stars), and the name of the reviewer. File the cards by title or subject.

Claudette Hegel, Bloomington, Minnesota
Library Media Connection • February 2003 (Volume 21, Issue 5)

Using Ads to "Sell" Books

Buy some clear plastic frames that stand up on their own (like easels) and in one of them put a recent full page-ad for a book or series you wish to promote. Put it on top of the fiction section where those books are shelved and stand or scatter several of the books near the framed ad. Those books will be checked out much more than before you displayed that ad!

Julia Steger, Clifton Middle School, Covington, Virginia
Library Media Connection • February 2003 (Volume 21, Issue 5)

Star Reviewers

We have a section on our school Web site called "Star Student Reviews." Students briefly describe their favorite book. I type their comments, take the student's picture with the book, and post it on our site. This has generated a lot of positive response and encouraged reading. (If students don't have written parental permission to have their picture on the Web, I type only the comments.) **http://www.gpisd.org/%7Ejackson//library/studentrev.htm**

Katie Sessler, Jackson Middle School Library, Grand Prairie, Texas
Library Media Connection • April/May 2004 (Volume 22, Issue 7)

Question of the Month

Every month I have a QUESTION OF THE MONTH. I post the question (with graphics from Print Shop) in the library and around school. It is also announced on the P.A. system. The question can be categorized as:

- Seasonal-Do vampire bats really suck blood?
- Current Events-Who is the leader of China?
- Related to a Topic a Teacher is Teaching-Match the author to his or her literary works.
- Curiosity-Why do penguins have fur instead of feathers? What causes hiccups? How come neon glows?
- Specific Subject Area-How many different life forms exist on Earth? How far does light travel in a nanosecond?

Students write their name, homeroom number, and answer on a small slip of paper. A winner is drawn at the end of the month by a student in the library for study hall or research. If the first slip drawn has the wrong answer, we keep drawing names until we get a slip with the correct answer. We have only one winner per month. Prizes include nail polish, soap on a rope, a fun pencil, and a gift certificate to a fast food restaurant.

Sue Dwars, Andrean High School, Merrillville, Indiana
Library Talk • March/April 2000 (Volume 13, Issue 2)

U T I L I Z I N G
TECHNOLOGY

What's New in the Library Media Center?

It is difficult to get information to students on new books, sequels, or just good books to read. At our middle school, we videotape morning announcements and show them during advisory/homeroom each day. One or two times a week we feature "What's New in the Library Media Center." Students read book reviews, list new arrivals or sequels, or feature current displays in the library media center. Students also get a glimpse of what the new books look like. Is it effective? Often the showcased book will be gone before advisory period is over!

Karen Reiber, Nagel Middle School, Cincinnati, Ohio
Library Media Connection • January 2006 (Volume 24, Issue 4)

Boost Your Professional Library

To boost your professional library, announce your new arrivals. While cataloging, create an annotated list of the new professional books, take a digital picture of the new books on the shelf, and send the list and photo to the entire staff in an e-mail. The teachers can read the list and description of each new book before they come to the library and know which books they are interested in beforehand. Teachers can even e-mail you and ask you to hold a certain book on the list for them! You might also add the photo and list to your media center link on the school's Web site, making the list available permanently for reference.

Ellen Proefrock, Lafayette-Winona Middle School, Norfolk, Virginia
Library Media Connection • April/May 2006 (Volume 24, Issue 7)

Videotaping as a Tool in the Classroom

During the first week of school, the seventh-grade English classes fill out a short reading survey of 10 questions such as: the kinds of books you like to read, your favorite authors, and the last book you read. Their teacher shares the answers with me. I have a booklist of quality authors and titles by genre that I attach to their survey. If they like R.L. Stine or horror, for example, I recommended books by Lois Duncan or Paul Zindel's *Loch or Doom Stone*. The second week, students come to the library for orientation. I do quick talks on books from various genres. A large selection of books is put on a cart from which the students may choose. While reading their book, they choose an exciting part or section that illustrates the tone of the book. Meanwhile, students have been paired in English class. Each interviews the other noting vital statistics, likes, dislikes, pets, interests, and hobbies. Once again they come to the library, and we videotape them at a microphone introducing their partner. They are encouraged to be creative in their introductions. The interviewer tells what book the partner has chosen. Their partner then reads aloud a selection from the book. That student then introduces the other partner. They have an opportunity to view the tapes in class. The videotaping is a great alternative to a traditional book report.

Diane C. Pozar, Walkill (New York) Middle School
The Book Report • March/April 2000 (Volume 18, Issue 5)

BUILDING
POSITIVE PUBLIC
RELATIONS

Savvy school librarians know that their actions are always being observed by numerous audiences: students, teachers, staff, and community members. To everyone else, the librarian is the library. Building on this awareness, librarians work to build positive feelings toward the school library with all segments of the public through personal interaction, thoughtful gestures, special events, programs, and utilizing visual and audio-visual modes of new and not-so-new technology.

This section addresses:

- Teachers and Staff
- Students
- Parents and Community
- Special Events
- Bookmarks and Booktalks

TEACHERS
AND STAFF

Media Center Cafe Holiday Luncheon

Try having a potluck luncheon on the last day of school before the winter holiday break. Everyone brings a dish to share, and you can order several hams and turkeys. Decorate the media center and organize all of the food. You can share recipes as well. This is purely social, but it creates great networking opportunities and a positive sense of camaraderie. It's an effective way of touching base with all departments in a non-pressured way.

Janet Rowland, Brecksville-Broadview Heights (Ohio) High School
Library Media Connection • November/December 2003 (Volume 22, Issue 3)

Staff Goodwill

We have found that one way to build goodwill with your staff members is through their stomachs! We usually provide treats for the whole staff in the library a couple times a year. One time is usually in observance of School Library Month in April. For example, insert bananas that have written on them, "This banana is due in the library Friday between 11 a.m. and 1 p.m.," into staff mailboxes. Then make banana splits when staff members bring in their bananas. We have also put large plastic cups in mailboxes and attached a note inviting staff members to bring the cup in at a certain time. We then served Italian sodas (this was a big hit!). This year we used paper "boats" and inserted a sail-shaped note that invited staff to "Sail into the Library for a Treat!" We then served strawberry shortcake with angel food cake.

Rosemary Knapp, Camas (Washington) High School
The Book Report • September/October 2000 (Volume 19, Issue 2)

Library Open House

During semester work days, offer a Library Open House for teachers, secretaries, custodians, staff, and administrators. To inform of the event, post flyers by the teacher mailboxes, on the bulletin board, in the weekly newsletter, and put notes in conspicuous places. For the open house, display new books in the library grouped by Dewey category. Provide lots of snacks, finger foods, and candy for treats, and enter everyone for door prizes. Include prizes such as note pads, fancy pens, posters, mouse pads, disk storage boxes, and so on. The door prize slips also document how many people attend.

 Janice Gumerman, Bingham Seventh Grade Center, Independence, Missouri
Library Media Connection • January 2004 (Volume 22, Issue 4)

Library Newsletter

We produce a media center newsletter for teachers, but because our time is limited, we have enlisted the aid of the desktop publishing class. I write the articles, save them to a disk, and give them to the desktop publishing teacher. Students work in groups of two or three to create the newsletter, adding graphics and headlines. The newsletters are given to me so that I can select one or more to use as the finished product. The class enjoys the practicality of the assignment, and I get a well-done newsletter. I then provide a treat for all class members as a thank you. Everyone is happy!

 Donna Paltzer, Xavier High School, Appleton, Wisconsin
The Book Report • May/June 2000 (Volume 19, Issue 1)

Thanks for Holding Down the Fort

This past Secretary's Day, I made a fort from my childhood set of Lincoln Logs. The center flag said "Media Center"; the corner flags said "Martha" and "Cheryl," the names of the secretaries who do so much to hold down the fort at our busy media center. The display was a great conversation piece and a unique way to celebrate Secretary's Day.

Mary Alice Anderson, Winona (Minnesota) Middle School
The Book Report • January/February 2000 (Volume 18, Issue 4)

Recognizing Library Users

At the end of each grading period, I place stars bearing individual teacher's last names in the faculty lounge. These can be placed on the wall or on each mailbox. I do this to recognize the teachers who used the library in some way, for example, by bringing classes in or checking out various items. And somewhere in the lounge I put a big sign proclaiming the "Library Superstars." Thank-you notes and candy in mailboxes is another way to recognize library usage.

Rosemary Sackleh, Lexington (Kentucky) Catholic High School
The Book Report • May/June 2000 (Volume 19, Issue 1)

Love, Your Media Center

For Valentine's Day, make a valentine for each staff member. Include chocolate and a note saying that you appreciate their support and participation in the media program. Sign the valentine, "Love, from your media center." It's a great "warm fuzzy."

Janet Rowland, Brecksville-Broadview Heights High School,
    Broadview Heights, Ohio
Library Media Connection • January 2005 (Volume 23, Issue 4)

Faculty Holiday Party

For Christmas, host a tea party for the faculty and staff. Hold it very early in December with the theme: "Join us for a Cup of Christmas Tea." Your computer teacher can create prettily decorated invitations. Invite faculty and staff to drop in during their free time in the afternoon. We decorated an adjoining conference room (allowing us to remain open for students throughout the afternoon) as a Christmas tea room with soft lighting, a small lit Christmas tree, lace tablecloths, and assorted china teacups (our own). Play holiday music quietly and light scented candles. Display Christmas and holiday books for browsing and borrowing. We bake an assortment of cookies and tea breads to go with a variety of flavored teas. Be sure to have printed copies of your recipes available.

 Bonnie Kelly, Magnificat High School, Rocky River, Ohio
Library Media Connection • November/December 2005 (Volume 24, Issue 3)

STUDENTS

PR Posters

Since we all know you can never have enough PR (or time between classes!), I let my sixth grade classes do poster projects to create PR for the titles of our state student book award nominees. Each group of 3-4 took one book, read reviews of it, and designed posters to advertise that title. We then displayed them around the school. A side benefit was increased circulation with our poster designers!

Mary Elizabeth Butcher, Mt. Vernon (Indiana) Junior High School
Library Talk • September/October 2000 (Volume 13, Issue 4)

Cafeteria for Advertising

I have found that one of the best places to post library informational items, such as new library books, the library happenings, or a book sale, is in the cafeteria where students stand in line waiting for food.

Patricia Kolencik, North Clarion High School, Tionesta, Pennsylvania
The Book Report • May/June 2000 (Volume 19, Issue 1)

Creative Menus

Our school district used popular author names in the menus during National Library Week, such as Faulkner salad or Shakespeare pudding. In the cafeteria, I displayed books by the authors whose names appeared on the menu. We had trivia questions each day from the books on display. Students received prizes of popular CDs, disks, reading posters, books, money, and ice cream.

Rosa James-Alston, Bruton High School, Williamsburg, Virginia
The Book Report • January/February 2001 (Volume 19, Issue 4)

You Oughta Be in Pictures

To promote books and technology, use your digital camera to take pictures of students reading a book, newspaper, or magazine during National Library Week in April. After cropping and labeling each picture with "National Library Week" and the date, insert them into mouse pads located by the computers in the library media center. Students love to see themselves in pictures!

Mary N. Stallings, Poquoson (Virginia) High School
The Book Report • March/April 2002 (Volume 20, Issue 5)

Faith in the Future

Some library patrons have a rocky, normal adolescence, but also seem to have great promise. When I see one of these students (alone, not with their entourage) I say sincerely, "When you are a successful businessperson, will you come back and donate a book to our library?" Of course I substitute whatever career seems likely: politician, artist, chef, or highway patrolperson. It's amazing what this vote of confidence does to melt and mend. It also says I believe in them in a way that a mere compliment about clothing, hair, or other attribute cannot.

Sheryl Kindle Fullner, Nooksack Valley Middle School, Everson, Washington
Library Media Connection • April/May 2005 (Volume 23, Issue 7)

PARENTS
AND COMMUNITY

Getting Parents into the Library

To get more parents to visit the Library Media Center on conference days, post the schedule of events and times inside each door with directions to the Library Media Center; hold registration or refreshments in the Library Media Center; schedule student readings of poetry or creative writing; present Reader's Theatre performed by students; display student-made art or curriculum projects; create new book displays and/or theme centers; hold mini concerts from band, choir, and orchestra; invite teams holding student-led conferences to use your warm and inviting facility. Remember, if their kids are involved, they'll come...sometimes even grandma and Aunt Gertie.

Candace R. Miller, Taft Middle School, Marion, Ohio
Library Media Connection • April/May 2004 (Volume 22, Issue 7)

Literacy Packet

A parent activity that does not involve asking for money can be a literacy packet for all 6th grade parents attending parent/teacher conferences. Put in the packet lists of best books from previous years, a bookmark, a flyer about the state supported information databases, information about public library programs, lists of book reviews, Internet sites for reading, etc. Go around to all of the classes before the conferences and tell the students if their parents came to the library to pick up a packet, the student will get a chance to win a free book from their homeroom. This provides some incentive for the student to encourage the parents to come to the library. Parents can also sign up for best book updates by leaving their email addresses. After the first of the year send them the links for the new best books for the current year. This activity is a quick, easy way to promote the library and meet some of the parents.

Mary Ann Reese, Central Middle School, Xenia, Ohio
Library Media Connection • November/December 2005 (Volume 24, Issue 3)

Donor Ideas

Metal and canvas folding chairs often go on sale in September. These are not the old style director's chairs, but ones that are used for camping and sports. They come with their own bags. On open house night, display items such as these canvas lounge chairs that parents can buy for the library. Next to the display put a large envelope with the store's name written prominently on it. The parents put money or a check into the envelope. On the canvas chairs you can ink in the name of the donor with a permanent fine point marker.

Sheryl Fullner, Nooksack Valley Middle School, Everson, Washington
Library Media Connection • November/December 2005 (Volume 24, Issue 3)

Open House

On open house night, for parents, the librarian offers free plastic bags with local bookstore advertising to hold all the teacher handouts. The bags make it more likely that the handouts will make it home. Besides, parents love getting something for free.

Peggy Fleming, Churchville-Chili Senior High School, Churchville, New York
The Book Report • November/December 2000 (Volume 19, Issue 3)

Promoting the LMC Web Address

Have the library media center Web address printed on bookmarks, fliers, brochures, newsletters, business cards, and other forms of printed materials. Send bookmarks home with students. Offer the business cards to administrators, community members, parents, and other educators. Staff members may also want business cards to hand out.

Debra Kay Logan, Mt. Gilead (Ohio) High School
Library Media Connection • March 2005 (Volume 23, Issue 6)

A Lifesaving Tip

At open houses for parents in our 10-12 building, I hand out 5 packs of lifesavers with a sign behind me that says "Librarians are life-savers at research paper time."

Peggy Fleming, Churchville-Chili Senior High, Churchville, New York
Library Media Connection • October 2004 (Volume 23, Issue 2)

SPECIAL
EVENTS

Library Homecoming

When our high school held its homecoming weekend, I asked the eight homecoming court girls and their escorts to bring in a 5 by 7 picture of themselves (most had had their senior pictures taken) and to tell me their favorite library book. The court's photos and accompanying books were featured in the lobby display case. Information about the student and the book was featured daily on the morning announcements. It was a great promotion for the students, the library, and reading!

Christine Nowicki, Montoursville (Pennsylvania) Area High School
The Book Report • November/December 2002 (Volume 21, Issue 3)

Read My Shirt

Our annual activity for National Library Week is "Read My Shirt" day on Friday. Use the library bulletin board to promote this activity. Put signs made on a color printer on big t-shirt shapes cut out of poster board. The shirts might have a poem or read "National Poetry Month," "April 11 is Read My Shirt Day," and "What will your shirt say?" but there are lots of possibilities.

Lucinda Deatsman, Mansfield SR. High School, Cline Ave. Campus, Mansfield, Ohio
Library Media Connection • March 2004 (Volume 22, Issue 6)

Poetry Festival

In the month of April (Poetry month), sponsor a Poetry Festival. Have students and teachers read their original work or their favorite poem. Serve refreshments and invite classes to come into the library.

 Mercedes Smith, Bishop Kenny High School, Jacksonville, Florida
The Book Report • January/February 2001 (Volume 19, Issue 4)

National Library Week

For National Library Week this year, we focused on libraries in movies. Yahoo yielded several pages of titles with brief annotations. A group of students marked those films with which they were familiar. We chose the top six, and the student assistants formulated questions they put on poster boards around the library. The names of the students with all correct answers were put into a raffle for a gift certificate to the movies. This contest attracted much participation from the students and enlivened our week

 Sister Alma Marie Walls, Our Lady of Lourdes Academy, Miami, Florida
The Book Report • November/December 2000 (Volume 19, Issue 3)

Appreciate Your Patrons

Consider thanking all the people who use your media center by having an appreciation week for teachers, students, or administrators. The week could include serving snacks at an informal social, showcasing the different services your media center offers, and showcasing and previewing library materials. You could offer small tokens of thanks such as bookmarks, pens, water bottles, etc. This is your way of making your patrons feel special and encouraging new patrons to see what the media center is all about. Be sure to advertise this event with bright, colorful flyers or daily announcements, or make a commercial promoting the event during announcements or Channel One time.

 Mercedes Smith, Bishop Kenny High School, Jacksonville, Florida
Library Talk • May/June 2002 (Volume 15, Issue 3)

Author Visit Memories

When an author visits, ask the students who have purchased books for signing to let you take a picture of them with the author. If you take these with a digital camera, it is very easy to take the memory stick to a store that makes prints and well worth the inexpensive cost of each picture. Give the individual pictures to the students and encourage them to glue the picture in the book that was purchased. This helps to preserve a lasting memory of this special occasion and is good public relations for the library program.

Janice Gumerman, Bingham Middle School, Independence, Missouri
Library Media Connection • April/May 2006 (Volume 24, Issue 7)

Welcoming an Author

Hosting an author for an overnight visit? Provide him or her with an inexpensive welcome bag or basket that contains some snacks, bottled water, and a magazine or current newspaper. Include your phone number and suggestions for close places to eat if the author will be on his or her own for any meals. Your thoughtfulness will make your out-of-town guest feel at home.

Pat Miller, Austin Parkway School Library, Sugar Land, Texas
Library Media Connection • March 2004 (Volume 22, Issue 6)

BOOKMARKS
AND BOOKTALKS

Promotional Bookmarks

As a library promotion, design a colorful bookmark for your library, with contact information, library logo, and a quote from a book. Or, as a contest, have classes compete for the best bookmark design, with the winner getting a free book or other suitable recognition. For long-lasting bookmarks, laminate them, and add a tassel to a punched hole.

Ava Goldman, California Public Employees' Retirement System,
    Sacramento, California
The Book Report • March/April 2002 (Volume 20, Issue 5)

TV Booktalk

Our school broadcasts school announcements via closed-circuit TV. Every Monday, I recruit a staff member or student to do a short booktalk, called "Get It, Read It" for this announcement program. This is an easy library promotion to organize and maintain, yet it publicizes the IMC collection and demonstrates the "reading" nature of a range of district employees and students.

Valerie Edwards, Monona Grove High School, Monona, Wisconsin
The Book Report • November/December 2001 (Volume 20, Issue 3)

Hi-Tech Booktalks

Besides placing new books in display cases, take digital pictures of high interest titles and "book talk" them via your closed circuit television system during daily broadcasts. After taking attractive pictures of the titles (colorful book covers, especially those of well-known personalities, e.g. Tiger Woods, work best), write short booktalks to accompany the photos. A "techie" student can then download the pictures to the master monitor while another student does the "voice over" of the booktalk. Show the book covers slowly, one dissolving into another, as the student speaks. This collaborative advertising effort reaches all students and staff members, resulting in increased book circulation and great PR.

 Richard McMahon, Center Line (Michigan) High School
Library Media Connection • October 2003 (Volume 22, Issue 2)

WORKING
WITH
HELPERS

Who among us does not need extra help? Student helpers and volunteers not only lighten our load, they often promote our emotional well being. Students who work as library aides and library assistants are usually a special joy because they help us informally keep in touch with the student population from the point of view of "one of them." Without them, we might run the risk of becoming misanthropic and jaded.

In addition to their contributions to our morale, these very special students can be a lifesaver to the school librarian who needs help with the ordinary mundane tasks of managing the library and trying to keep things in order while also doing all the special things we want to do.

Volunteers likewise may provide us with glimpses of the outside world, help with clerical and other library-related work, and often promote positive public relations for us.

Tips in this section are divided into two categories:
- Students
- Volunteers

STUDENTS

Staff Badges

Library Aide pins are costly, difficult to pin on, and most of all unhip. We collected lanyards with ID pockets from various conferences and designed colorful inserts for our student workers. Easy and cool and free.

Sheryl Fullner, Nooksack Valley Middle School, Everson, Washington
Library Media Connection • March 2006 (Volume 24, Issue 6)

Efficient E-mails

I collected my student aides' e-mail addresses so I can send them notes of things I've forgotten to tell them, as well as reminders when they forget to bring in necessary paperwork.

Anitra Gordon, Lincoln High School, Ypsilanti, Michigan
The Book Report • March/April 2002 (Volume 20, Issue 5)

Start a Library Club

All of our library assistants are invited to join the Library Club, which meets once a month during the regular school year. Club meetings provide an opportunity for group training, as well as creating friendships among the assistants.

Arlene Kachka, Resurrection High School, Chicago, Illinois
The Book Report • May/June 2002 (Volume 21, Issue 1)

Reading Shelves

Reading the shelves is essential to keep the library media center from chaos, but skilled student or parent volunteers for this task are few and far between. Several times a year, I print out my shelf list after sorting according to call number. It is a job that takes less than five minutes (the printing takes longer of course). Then student clerks or other volunteers, working in pairs, can easily make the shelves match the shelf-order sheet. This eliminates the need to train.

 Sheryl Fullner, Nooksack Valley Middle School, Everson, Washington
Library Media Connection • October 2005 (Volume 24, Issue 2)

Check Your Library Shelvers' Accuracy

Before helpers arrive, take five books from the shelving cart (choosing a wide variety of the most difficult) and hold them so that their spines all face down. Photocopy the five spines at once. Keep the photocopy on your desk and after the suspect shelver has come and gone, check the whereabouts of those five books. If there are any problems, pull the books and discuss the fine points with the helper whose name you put on the photocopy along with the date. Make sure this is not an accusatory conference. It should be more along the lines of, "I've noticed you have a little difficulty with double digit decimals. Let's see if we can make a cheat sheet to help you." The review is helpful, but those little words "I've noticed" coupled with the actual photocopy helps folks know that accountability is required.

 Sheryl Kindle Fullner, Nooksack Valley Middle School, Everson, Washington
The Book Report • March/April 2002 (Volume 20, Issue 5)

Library Aide Photos as Wallpaper

Take photos of all of your library aides with a digital camera, then use the photos as wallpaper on your computers.

Anitra Gordon, Lincoln High School, Ypsilanti, Michigan
The Book Report • May/June 2002 (Volume 21, Issue 1)

Checking Shelvers

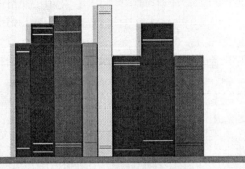

We have our student helpers follow a particular method when shelving books: we ask that they place books pages-side-down on the shelf, so that the books' spines are facing up and are parallel with the floor. Then we check the shelves. Using this method makes it easy to spot the books that were just shelved. If a book is in the right place, we stand it up properly. If not, it's taken back to the book cart, and the student reshelves it. If there's a persistent problem with a helper's work, we go to the shelves with that student and explain and demonstrate how the books should be shelved. Then we have the student shelve while we watch, and we offer help if it's needed.

Mary Drexler, JCB High School, Phoenix, New York
The Book Report • September/October 2002 (Volume 21, Issue 2)

VOLUNTEERS

Training Volunteers

To help parent volunteers, I type up instruction sheets for our most common tasks: creating and applying a spine label, stamping or putting labels on media, covering book jackets with mylar. These instruction sheets include a list of needed materials and tools, step-by-step instructions, and a sample of the finished product. The sheets are then laminated or slipped into a clear plastic sleeve. All of the sheets have one bold face statement at the bottom: "Grateful for your help in providing library materials that are tidy and uniform." The sheets have minimized my training time for each volunteer.

Sheryl Kindle Fullner, Nooksack Valley Middle School, Everson, Washington
Library Media Connection • April/May 2004 (Volume 22, Issue 7)

Aroma Bookmarkers

Many magazines have fragrance samples. Volunteers can easily trim off the magazine pages and put the samples in a bookmark bin at the checkout desk. Some magazines have as many as four per issue. We mark each with a male or female symbol; once it is cut from the ad, it may be hard to visually distinguish. This process actually makes the magazines more accessible to allergen-sensitive students without overly perfuming the books into which they are placed. These bookmarks are very popular with our students.

Sheryl Kindle Fullner, Nooksack Valley Middle School, Everson, Washington
Library Media Connection • January 2005 (Volume 23, Issue 4)

Laminated Instructions

To make sure that my parent volunteers always know what to do and how to do it, I laminated instructions and taped them to the top of the circulation desk. One sheet lists all the duties of the parent volunteers. The other sheet has step-by-step instructions for checking books in, out, and renewing them. I made them in Print Shop so they look nice. The checkout instructions are handy for the student assistants, too.

Yapha Nussbaum Mason, Brentwood School Library, Los Angeles, California
The Book Report • January/February 2001 (Volume 19, Issue 4)

Fast Reading Level

There are many online sites that publish reading levels; however, I often run across a book not listed. I quickly type a paragraph into a Word document and hit spell check. At the end of spell check, the Flesch-Kincaid Reading level appears. This process takes less than a minute and can also be done by student or parent helpers.

Sheryl Kindle Fullner, Nooksack Valley Middle School, Everson, Washington
Library Media Connection • January 2006 (Volume 24, Issue 4)

Personalized Holiday Gifts for Parent Volunteers

In November, call the children of your parent volunteers in to the library and take each child's photo with a digital camera. Ask the children to write down a special memory or tradition that their family takes part in during their holiday season. Once you have their words and photo, put the two together in a narrow column format—about the size of a bookmark—print each one with color ink, and have each one laminated. As a final touch, punch a hole in the top and tie a ribbon through the hole. Your parent volunteers will be touched by what their children write, and the final product can be used as a bookmark or a holiday ornament.

Laura Stiles, Cedar Valley Middle School, Austin, Texas
Library Media Connection • November/December 2005 (Volume 24, Issue 3)

MANAGING
TIPS FOR THE
LIBRARIAN

Don't forget that the most important aspect of the library program is you! Your health and happiness are essential to a workable library. Take time to be healthy. Leave the library occasionally to attend conferences. Read professional books like this one to hone your skills. Pat yourself on the back for the work you do. Your job is the most important job in the world!

Library Fitness

As librarians, we have access to more health information than anyone in our nation, yet many of us are sedentary. A great New Year's resolution is to be more active. When walking in school hallways, pick up the pace, and swing your arms. Instead of sending student helpers on long distance errands, let them mind the desk and take the trek yourself. I have used a pedometer to map our school with a goal of walking 2 miles in the course of the workday. My improved efficiency and energy levels more than make up for the brief amount of time I am away from the circ or reference desk.

 Sheryl Fullner, Nooksack Valley Middle School, Everson, Washington
Library Media Connection • November/December 2005 (Volume 24, Issue 3)

Pen on a Rope

I was always misplacing my pen until I got a "pen on a rope," which I wear around my neck every day. Now I always have a pen handy.

 Meg Miranda, Highland View Middle School, Corvallis, Oregon
The Book Report • January/February 2000 (Volume 18, Issue 4)

Stick 'em Up!

When you attend a conference or workshop, take a roll of self-stick address labels with you. This helps when filling out door prize slips, request for information cards for vendors, or even exchanging contact information with other participants. Also more legible than hastily scrawled hand written materials.

 Janice Gumerman, Bingham Seventh Grade Center, Independence, Missouri
Library Media Connection • November/December 2003 (Volume 22, Issue 3)

ABOUT THE EDITOR

Sherry York, a retired school librarian, is married to a retired school librarian. Together they worked for a combined total of more than sixty years as educators. During those years they collaborated on many library-related projects and shared numerous tips.

Since retirement Sherry has worked as a reviewer, conference presenter, indexer, and Linworth project editor. She has written reviews, articles, author profiles, and bibliographies for *The Book Report, Library Talk,* and *Library Media Connection.* She continues to review for *LMC* and for *VOYA (Voice of Youth Advocates).*

She is the author of four Linworth books on multicultural literature:

- *Picture Books by Latino Writers: A Guide for Librarians, Teachers, Parents, and Students* (2002)
- *Children's and Young Adult Literature by Latino Writers: A Guide for Librarians, Teachers, Parents, and Students* (2002)
- *Children's and Young Adult Literature by Native Americans: A Guide for Librarians, Teachers, Parents, and Students* (2003)
- *Ethnic Book Awards: A Directory of Multicultural Literature for Young Readers* (2005)

Sherry and her husband Donnie live on a subtropical island in South Texas, where he manages a reading room and she maintains a flexible schedule. Recently she has been a judge for the Publishers Marketing Association and for the WILLA (Women Writing the West) awards. She reads mysteries indiscriminately and utilizes technology to expand her lengthy to-read list. Books in their personal library need weeding, and their shelves are not in order!

TIPS
OF YOUR OWN

T**I**P**s**

OF YOUR OWN